Renaissance Poetry

Edited by Duncan Wu

Blackwell
Publishing

Copyright © 2002 by Blackwell Publishers Ltd,
a Blackwell Publishing company

Editorial arrangement and introduction copyright © 2002 by Duncan Wu

350 Main Street, Malden, MA 02148–5018, USA
108 Cowley Road, Oxford OX4 1JF, UK
550 Swanston Street, Carlton South, Victoria 3053, Australia
Kurfürstendamm 57, 10707 Berlin, Germany

First published 2002 by Blackwell Publishers Ltd

Library of Congress Cataloging-in-Publication Data

Renaissance poetry / edited by Duncan Wu.
p. cm. – (Blackwell essential literature)
Includes bibliographical references and index.
ISBN 0-631-23009-2 (alk. paper) – ISBN 0-631-23010-6 (pbk.: alk. paper)
1. English poetry–Early modern, 1500–1700. I. Wu, Duncan. II. Series.
PR1207 .R46 2002   821'.308–dc21
2002022322

A catalogue record for this title is available from the British Library.

Set in 8/10pt Galliard
by Kolam Information Services Pvt. Ltd, Pondicherry, India
Printed and bound in the United Kingdom by T.J. International, Padstow, Cornwall

For further information on
Blackwell Publishing, visit our website:
http://www.blackwellpublishing.com

Contents

Michael Drayton (1563–1631)   43

Christopher Marlowe (1564–1593)   44

William Shakespeare (1564–1616)   45

Ben Jonson (?1573–1637)   79

Robert Herrick (1591–1674)   97

Henry King (1592–1669)   102

George Herbert (1593–1633)   105

Series Editor's Preface

The Blackwell Essential Literature series offers readers the chance to possess authoritative texts of key poems (and in one case drama) across the standard periods and movements. Based on correspondent volumes in the Blackwell Anthologies series, most of these volumes run to no more than 200 pages. The acknowledged virtues of the Blackwell Anthologies are range and variety; those of the Essential Literature series are authoritative selection, compactness and ease of use. They will be particularly helpful to students hard-pressed for time, who need a digest of the poetry of each historical period.

In selecting the contents of each volume particular attention has been given to major writers whose works are widely taught at most schools and universities. Each volume contains a general introduction designed to introduce the reader to those central works.

Together, these volumes comprise a crucial resource for anyone who reads or studies poetry.

Duncan Wu
St Catherine's College, Oxford

Acknowledgements

I thank my colleagues at St Catherine's College, Jeremy Dimmick and Andy Eburne, and Richard McCabe of Merton College, for advice during work on this volume. I have also been the grateful recipient of guidance from my friend and former colleague, Professor Philip Hobsbaum of the University of Glasgow. Preparation of the volume led me to exploit the resources of various Oxford libraries – in particular I thank Sally Collins and Shaun Belcher of St Catherine's College Library and Mr A. Ricketts of St Peter's College Library.

Introduction

Duncan Wu

The historical period covered by this volume – 1590 to 1660, or there-abouts – hardly amounts to a coherent one, and can only partly justify the title of 'Renaissance' (which probably began towards the beginning of the sixteenth century). But it does contain some of the most important poets in the canon of Renaissance literature. It has been the site of some of the most vigorous literary research of recent years, which brought to notice a number of neglected writers. Various anthologies have reflected these advances, not least Robert Cummings's *Seventeenth-Century Poetry* in the Blackwell Annotated Anthologies series.[1] Given the ready availability of 'canon-breakers', there seems little point in repeating their achievements within the small scale provided by this series, so as with the *Romantic Poetry* volume I have preferred to address the achievements of 'major' poets of the period, representing them as fully as space allows. As always, I have preferred not to extract from longer works except where no option presents itself; such is the case with *The Faerie Queene*.

Spenser began publishing *The Faerie Queene* in 1596. His great work was written in a stanza of his own device, which has the power of accommodating the vast range of newly minted words in the language, and exploiting to the full their rhythm and music. It is an epic work that looks back to the epics of folklore, the Arthurian legends, and the poetry of Virgil, Homer, Ariosto and Tasso. In essence it is concerned with virtues of various kinds – love, faith, friendship – in allegorical form. Each virtue has its own knight or protector, and in Gloriana (the Faerie Queene) Spenser presents the glory that results from the possession of virtue. The poem has a political message too, as Gloriana represents Elizabeth I to whom Spenser was devoted.

In July 1820, while waiting for his last volume of poems to be published, Keats marked up a copy of *The Faerie Queene* for Fanny Brawne, indicating his favourite passages; the task, he told her, 'has lightened my time very much'. He would have directed her attention to at least some, if not all, of the passages here – including the bower of bliss (see pp. 16–20, below). It was among those singled out by Hazlitt in his lectures on the English poets, where he remarked:

---

[1] Others include *The Penguin Book of Renaissance Verse 1509–1659* ed. H. R. Woudhuysen, introduced by David Norbrook (Harmondsworth: Penguin Books, 1993), *The New Oxford Book of Sixteenth-Century Verse* ed. Emrys Jones (Oxford 1992), and *The New Oxford Book of: Oxford University Press, Seventeenth-Century Verse* ed. Alastair Fowler (Oxford: Oxford University Press, 1992).

In Spenser, we wander in another world, among ideal beings. The poet takes and lays us in the lap of a lovelier nature, by the sound of softer streams, among greener hills and fairer valleys. He paints nature not as we find it, but as we expected to find it, and fulfils the delightful promise of our youth. He waves his wand of enchantment – and at once embodies airy beings, and throws a delicious veil over all actual objects. The two worlds of reality and of fiction are poised on the wings of his imagination.

Both Spenser and his contemporary, Sir Walter Ralegh, could be described (to use Hazlitt's phrase) as spirits of the age – Ralegh more so than Spenser, as he won his Queen's favour to become, from about 1580 to 1592, one of the most powerful men in the country. His most famous work, 'The Nymph's Reply to the Shepherd' (p. 35) is a response to Marlowe's 'The Passionate Shepherd to his Love' (p. 44), and the two frequently appear together. Ralegh's poem is a memorable antidote to the romantic pastoral of Marlowe's; his nymph sees through the seductive unreality envisaged by Marlowe's shepherd, recognizing it as 'pretty' but ephemeral.

Fulke Greville, Lord Brooke, was also at court, and remained there until the reign of Charles I; in 1628 he was stabbed to death by a servant who believed he had been passed over in his will. His most important single collection of poems is *Caelica* (1633), most of which were written between about 1577 and 1600. I have selected principally from those of the middle to late part of that time, which reveal Greville at his most adventurous. Who but he could have framed what appears at first to be a love poem as a vision of death (in 'When all this All', p. 36), or have begun a poem about devotion to God with a terrifying portrayal of the end of the world ('The earth with thunder torn', p. 36)? Towards the end of *Caelica* Greville seems to foreshadow such poets as Herbert in the intensity with which he writes about Christian belief. 'Down in the depth of mine iniquity' (p. 37) is a prime example, where hell is an inner state of torment generated by the soul itself, but out of which comes, without warning, 'this saving God of mine'. That inner terror pervades the later poems, especially 'In night when colours all to black are cast' (p. 37), which speaks eloquently of the doings of the 'inward evils' of which he was all too conscious.

The first sonnet sequence in English, *Astrophil and Stella* (1591) was probably composed by another court poet, Sir Philip Sidney, between about November 1581 and late 1582. Sonnet cycles had been in fashion on the Continent for some time – either translated or imitated from originals by Petrarch. Sidney brought the vogue to England where it caught on, inspiring similar works by Spenser, Drayton and Shakespeare. *Astrophil and Stella* shows how flexible the sonnet form could be; while Sidney looked back to Petrarch, he was unafraid of writing sonnets in alexandrines. But the real achievement of the sequence is its exploration of Astrophil's psychology. As Katherine Duncan-Jones has observed, its 'true subject seems often to be not so much Astrophil's adoration of Stella as his inability to come to terms with his own inner self'. Even in those sonnets where he addresses a disapproving friend, the criticism could originate from within. The poetry is one of obsessive self-involution, and often reads as if Astrophil were speaking of himself to himself; 'I am not I; pity the tale of me'. But that, of course, is the nature of love – entwined as it can become with insecurity, depression and self-loathing.

As a dramatist, Marlowe's great achievement was the four tragedies written between 1587 and 1593 – *Tamburlaine the Great* (two parts), *Dr Faustus*, *The Jew of Malta* and *Edward II*. 'The Passionate Shepherd to his Love' remains his best-known poem, and the inspiration of the response offered by Ralegh's more down-to-earth 'Nymph'. Marlowe's poem was first published in 1599, six years after his early death in mysterious circumstances (he was stabbed to death at the inn of the widow Bull in Deptford). It was immediately popular, and sung in a garbled version by one of Shakespeare's characters, Sir Hugh Evans, in *The Merry Wives of Windsor*.

Though published in 1609, Shakespeare's 154 sonnets were probably written in the 1590s – scholars date them to the period 1592–6. They comprise a remarkable body of work, and had we only the sonnets Shakespeare would still be regarded as among the greatest of our poets. It is thought that the first 126 are addressed to a young man he loved, of superior beauty and rank but of questionable fidelity. Sonnets 127 to 152 comprise a less coherent group, involving a mistress of the poet's, the 'dark lady'. The last two, 153 and 154, are believed to be translations of a version of a Greek epigram. The form used by Shakespeare is that of the English sonnet developed by Surrey, of three quatrains and a couplet (the exceptions are 99, 126 and 145). The couplet is often the chief means by which he ties the poem into one of the central themes of the cycle – lust, time, the passing of youth. Because we cannot be certain of the correct order of the sonnets it is almost impossible to form a coherent, logical narrative out of them. In the end we are left with the shifting attitudes of the central speaker – the poet – towards his friends, lovers and, of course, himself.

In Keats's copy of the sonnets, one of the most heavily marked is number 64 – 'When I have seen by Time's fell hand defaced' – echoes of which rang in his head as he composed 'When I have fears that I may cease to be'. It is easy to see why Keats loved it: it is a prime example of how Shakespeare manages to harmonize the music and meaning of the language to create a powerful statement about loss.

> When I have seen by Time's fell hand defaced
>   The rich proud cost of outworn buried age;
> When sometime lofty towers I see down-rased,
>   And brass eternal slave to mortal rage ... (ll. 1–4)

The cadences of the verse, its reluctance to resolve, and the constant withholding of the end of the sentence, which remains suspended until as late as line 11, compel our attention. When it finally does resolve, the concluding couplet lives up to its promise.

> This thought is as a death, which cannot choose
> But weep to have that which it fears to lose.

That which it fears to lose? The sonnet is not just about loss, or even death – it's a love poem. And what it does so cleverly is to connect the insecurity of love with the knowledge of our own mortality. Each of the sonnets is just as precise and perceptive in its analysis of human psychology.

Donne may have waited until the early twentieth century for recognition because he was so uncompromisingly original that no one knew quite how to evaluate him – not just in his ideas but in his experiments with poetic form. This was no bookworm, nor stay-at-home. He was a man of action – a courtier, a member of Essex's expedition to Cadiz and the Azores (1596–7), secretary to Sir Thomas Egerton the Lord Keeper (a political post), MP for Brackley (1601) and Taunton (1614), a prisoner (for his secret marriage to his master's niece), and Dean of St Paul's – and his poetry is grounded in life as he lived it. By contrast with the generation of sonneteers that preceded him, he is known best for love lyrics that look back not to Petrarch but to classical writers such as Martial and Juvenal. Typically, the voice that speaks in his poems is that of the sceptic. He knows how short is the time given to him, and that pervades his comments on love and life.

> Just so much honour, when thou yield'st to me,
> Will waste, as this flea's death took life from thee. ('The Flea', ll. 26–7)

It is not just death that overshadows lovers' passions, but the questionable nature of love – something of which Donne is acutely conscious. In 'The Bait' the classical trope so fashionable at that time (and used with such success by Marlowe on p. 44) – 'Come live with me, and be my love' – gives way to an unexpectedly predatory vision. It cannot be that his lover's eyes warm the river more effectively than the sun – but where Sidney might have presented such an idea as a courtly conceit, Donne does so fully aware of its dangers. Indeed, if Donne's poem counts for anything at all, it is effective at evoking the precariousness of worldly affairs – the cutting of the anglers' legs leaves us in no doubt of it.

Donne is an insider in that he worked his way through the upper echelons of society to emerge as one of the most highly esteemed men of his day – but his perspective is also that of the outsider: he was a cradle Catholic and therefore, literally, excluded from many things (including taking a degree from Oxford) before in the 1590s he shed the religion into which he had been born. The fruit of this is his verse, which possesses the kind of sharp intelligence that makes the court poetry of his day seem cosily affirmative. At the same time, Donne is no less attentive to the psycho-logical reality of love-relationships than Sidney or Shakespeare, and no less expert at dramatizing it. Many of his poems open abruptly, like speeches from a play:

> 'Busy old fool, unruly sun . . .'
> ''Tis true, 'tis day; what though it be?'
> 'I wonder by my troth, what thou and I
> Did, till we loved?'

Donne's poems take for granted the fact that love gives way to loss and eventually to death. The poet of 'The Funeral' is already a corpse, and addresses the poem to both his lover and future mourners; in 'The Relic' he and his lover are long buried; and in 'A Nocturnal upon St Lucy's Day' he is 'every dead thing' – less than stones, trees and 'ordinary' nothings.

Ben Jonson had a preacher for a father and a bricklayer for a stepfather. Like the preacher and the bricklayer, he shows a deep concern in his work for 'order and disposure' as he put it. He wrote out the content of his poems in prose before turning to verse, a technique that helped him achieve the concentrated meaning enshrined in his epigrams. If the poetry is well cast and finely tuned, so was Jonson's vision. He was a latter-day stoic, believing in the power of God to see him through, wrapping intense emotions within linguistic and intellectual conceits. So it is that in 'On my First Son' he begins by punning on his son's name, Benjamin, with its Hebrew meaning of 'dextrous', before using the almost shocking mercantile image of the child being paid back to God:

> Seven years thou wert lent to me, and I thee pay,
> Exacted by thy fate, on the just day. (ll. 3–4)

That belief in a presiding order within the cosmos is reflected in his social and political vision of order so memorably described in 'To Penshurst'. The residence of Robert Sidney, Lord Lisle, brother to Sir Philip Sidney, Penshurst becomes the exemplar of good local government, embodying the virtues of just rule. Its walls 'are reared with no man's ruin, no man's groan;/There's none that dwell about them wish them down' (ll. 46–7). The ideal depends on its being humane and harmonized, from Sidney down to the lowest labourer. Even the fishes and the vegetable world partake of it. No proud, ambitious heap, the overblown residence of lords and ladies with no regard for the people around them and the environment they share, Penshurst is a place where 'thy lord dwells'. In that last line the concept of dwelling is redefined to signify the creation and preservation of political and social justice, something echoing the divine order implied in the elegies.

'I sing of brooks, of blossoms, birds, and bowers', wrote Herrick at the opening of *Hesperides* (1648). He favoured the small canvas – brief poems that focus on small domestic or natural vignettes. A friend of Jonson, Herrick filled *Hesperides* with 1,200 poems, many of them short, ranging across an impressive variety of literary forms – elegies, epitaphs, epigrams, hymns, songs and classical imitations. The pastoral content of many of these works doubtless owes much to the fact that he lived for a long time in Devon. The best of the pastoral verses – such as 'To Daisies' (p. 99) – avoid a merely emblematic use of natural images through a tender charm that owes something to the fact that they are a kind of erotic poem. Though usually thought of as a pastoral poet, Herrick's famous volume was published in the midst of the English Civil War, and some of his poems are laden with political anxiety. 'Ill Government', 'Kings and Tyrants' and 'The Difference betwixt Kings and subjects' bear on issues that arose prior to or during the War.

Henry King was a friend of Donne and an admirer of Jonson. 'The Exequy' is his finest work, and bears comparison with Jonson's 'On my First Son'. As in Jonson, the verse acts as a container for a grief so intense that it threatens constantly to overwhelm us – but never does. Its characteristic mode of operation is to offset the powerful emotion behind it by distancing King's dead wife – 'thou art the book, / The library whereon I look'; she becomes his 'clear sun', something 'I could not keep'. An exequy is in fact a procession – in this case that of the objects that reflect or enshrine King's grief. The reification of the loved object, while setting her at a distance, tells us more of his emotions than would a more direct utterance of loss.

George Herbert died before he was able to publish his poems; they appeared posthumously as *The Temple: Sacred Poems and Private Ejaculations* (1633), and went through 13 editions by 1680. It is one of the finest volumes of devotional poetry in the language, forging its own manner from the outset, characterized by carefully and intricately wrought patterns of imagery and language. As the book's subtitle indicates, Herbert's poems find expression at the point where private meditation intersects with public worship. To that end he enlists a range of skills – wit, passion, and his finely tuned dramatic sense. 'Love' is precisely such a work, in which Christ becomes a welcoming host, perhaps a lover. 'The Flower' maps the feelings of the believer and finds them similar to those of someone in love, fluctuating as the individual believes himself to be rejected and then, once more, welcomed. Throughout, one is aware of passionate feeling – 'I struck the board, and cried, "No more, / I will abroad"' ('The Collar', ll. 1–2). That passion owes something to the fact that Herbert's subject is belief – something more pressing than life itself. His poems are more than personal statements; they are about the life of the spirit, felt constantly to be under threat from enemies within and without.

If Herbert created dramas of the spirit, something similar might be said of John Milton. Even in the midst of an elegy for his Cambridge friend Edward King (*Lycidas*, 1638) he finds the opportunity to introduce St Peter, who compares the lamented Lycidas with the grasping shepherds of a corrupted English Church:

> What recks it them? What need they? They are sped;
> And when they list, their lean and flashy songs
> Grate on their scrannel pipes of wretched straw...(ll. 122–4)

It is a vision of corruption which foresees the creeping influence of Catholicism (the 'grim wolf' of l. 128) and the ultimate outbreak of civil war (the 'two-handed engine' of l. 130 – which is of course a sword). Milton's poetry develops its dramas, typically, on various levels.

Lycidas was Milton's first important poem. He had emerged from a London family and a troubled career at Cambridge (where he quarrelled with his tutor and was known as 'the Lady of Christ's'); he retired to the country shortly after, where he composed *L'Allegro* and *Il Penseroso*, which celebrate mirth and solitude respectively. Critics differ over whether the different realms they describe are complementary or stand in opposition.

In ensuing years he made a name for himself as a pamphleteer, writing in favour of divorce (after the failure of his own marriage to the 16-year-old Mary Powell), freedom of the press (in *Areopagitica*) and against the Established Church (in *The Reason of Church Government*). It is easy to think of poetry as a distraction from his true career, which took him into the political mainstream. His pamphlet in support of regicide in 1649 led to promotion by Cromwell to the post of Secretary of Foreign Tongues to the Council of State, which required him to translate diplomatic documents and correspondence. Marvell became his assistant in 1657. During these years he continued pamphleteering, intermittently writing poetry, mainly sonnets. He worked hard for the Commonwealth and was bitterly disappointed when it collapsed. His works burnt in the streets, he was hunted down and imprisoned with the expectation of a swift execution. But Charles II seems eventually to have relented (perhaps, it is said, at the entreaty of Andrew Marvell); he was released and spent his retirement in London composing *Paradise Lost* (which is covered by the volume *Poetry from 1660 to 1780* in this series).

In the context of his other writings, Milton's sonnets are a minor achievement. But later poets would regard them as innovatory – more so, in some respects, than his great epic. Those who followed in Sidney's footsteps tended to see the sonnet as ideally suited to love poetry. Milton's achievement was to look back to the other strand of thought in the Petrarchan tradition and understand its potential as a mode of political expression. (Petrarch had written sonnets denouncing the Roman Church.) Its influence has been enduring. There can be little doubt that Wordsworth would not have written sonnets in support of Toussaint L'Ouverture and in opposition to Napoleon in 1802 had it not been for Milton.

The earliest of the public sonnets was that 'On the Lord General Fairfax at the Siege of Colchester' (p. 123), which celebrates the military career of Sir Thomas Fairfax, one of the foremost commanders on the parliamentary side during the Civil War. 'To the Lord General Cromwell' (pp. 123–4), written in 1652, is preoccupied with Cromwell's work on the Committee for the Propagation of the Gospel, appointed to look into the payment of ministers and limits of religious toleration. Milton urges Cromwell to reject the idea of uniting civil and religious power ('secular chains') and a stipendiary clergy ('hireling wolves'). Sir Henry Vane the Younger (1613–62) was a statesman on the parliamentary side; Milton's sonnet to him refers to the treachery of Holland ('hollow states') and his opposition to the Established Church (ll. 10–11), a cause with which Milton sympathized. Partly in admiration of this poem, Wordsworth would refer to Vane in his own sonnet in praise of republicans past, 'Great men have been among us'. Milton's 'On the Late Massacre in Piedmont' is a lament for the Protestant Vaudois sect butchered by Charles Emmanuel II, Duke of Savoy, in 1655.

> Avenge, O Lord, thy slaughtered saints, whose bones
> Lie scattered on the Alpine mountains cold . . . (ll. 1–2)

Milton's passion is unmistakable, not just through the imperative mood of these lines, but in the repeated 'o' sound that tolls like a passing bell throughout the rest of the poem. He has traced his indignation back to a deeply felt grief, as is clear from his references to the Vaudois' 'martyred blood', blamed on that 'triple tyrant' the pope (who wore a tripletiered crown).

'For what can war but endless war still breed?' Milton asks in 'On the Lord General Fairfax' – a curious question to ask, given Milton's respect for Fairfax's soldiery. In expressing such anxieties Milton spoke for a whole class of middle-class Protestant dissenters that included Andrew Marvell, who during the 1650s served as tutor to Fairfax's daughter. Marvell was then in his thirties: the Civil War was at its height, and he was composing the poetry by which we know him today. The uncertainty and insecurity of Britain at war with itself colours his vision, whether he writes of affairs of state or of the spirit. Resolution seems impossible even in 'To his Coy Mistress', which ends not with the expected image of harmony but with one of war – that of a cannonball breaking through the gates of a fortress.

In 'Tom May's Death' (late 1650), Marvell places in Ben Jonson's mouth a credo we may identify as his own. When judges and 'coward churchmen' are too afraid to speak out,

> He, when the wheel of empire whirleth back,
> And though the world's disjointed axle crack,
> Sings still of ancient rights and better times,
> Seeks wretched good, arraigns successful crimes. (ll. 67–70)

Those 'ancient rights and better times' haunt Marvell's poetry because they were absent from the world in which he lived, caught up in the chaos and confusion of the Civil War and its bloody aftermath. And that fact made the poet's task much harder. For Marvell, the combination of humour with high seriousness was not just a matter of style – it was a survival strategy. Even today his attitude towards Cromwell in 'An Horatian Ode' remains a matter for debate. How, for instance, do we read the 'forward youth' in the first line – as Marvell or Cromwell? And what should we make of the sword which, in the poem's final lines, performs the role of a crucifix?

> The same arts that did gain
> A power, must it maintain. (ll. 119–20)

Marvell's sympathy for Charles I, the 'royal actor' on the 'tragic scaffold', is as pointed as his concern at the 'arts' that brought Cromwell to power, and which Cromwell, having just deployed them against the Irish (many of whose inhabitants he had recently slaughtered) was about to use, with equal ruthlessness, against the Scots.

'Upon Appleton House', a complete text of which is included in this volume, is set in the grounds of the estate of Marvell's then employer, Lord

General Thomas Fairfax (1612–71), until recently commander-in-chief of the parliamentary army (and chiefly responsible for the victory of the parliamentary side at Marston Moor). Disturbed by the execution of Charles I (though he had done nothing to prevent it), Fairfax resigned his commission in June 1650 in protest at Cromwell's campaign to suppress the Scots. He retired with his wife, Ann Vere, to Nun Appleton, a former Cistercian priory where in 1651 they appointed Marvell tutor to their daughter Mary; he would remain there for two years and composed 'Upon Appleton House' probably in summer 1651.

The poem finds Marvell preoccupied with Fairfax's withdrawal from public life; had he wished, Fairfax

> Might once have made our gardens spring
> Fresh as his own and flourishing. (ll. 347–8)

The mock battles played out in the grounds of Appleton House are more than a comic device; they hint gently at a disproportion that has led Fairfax to renounce his true calling (that of the soldier) for a false one – that of gardener. In so doing Fairfax has abandoned his true destiny. Marvell seems to imply that Fairfax might have offered a less turbulent administration from that of Cromwell: in his hands conduct of the war might have been less cataclysmic and led more speedily to a settled peace.

As in the 'Horatian Ode' Marvell is not afraid to disconcert, or allude to the miseries of war, particularly in the 'massacre' of the rails (corncrakes), and bloodthirsty glee of Thestylis at stanza 51.

> Where, as the meads with hay, the plain
> Lies quilted o'er with bodies slain:
> The women that with forks it fling
> Do represent the pillaging. (ll. 421–4)

Such violence is never far from Marvell's vision: soldiers shoot the nymph's fawn dead while the lovers of 'To His Coy Mistress' roll their love into a cannonball. It is part of a larger evil that pervades the fallen world, capable even of bringing into question the urge to write devotional poetry (in 'The Coronet'). By extension, as in 'A Dialogue Between the Soul and the Body', the body itself becomes the source of the problem. ''Tis not what once it was, the world, / But a rude heap together hurled': deep dismay at the postlapsarian universe accounts for the longing which Marvell feels for its opposite – the repose underpinning 'The Garden', 'On a Drop of Dew', 'The Coronet' and 'Bermudas'.

Marvell was not the only young man whose life was changed by the Civil War. His contemporary Henry Vaughan was studying to be a lawyer in London when it broke out and put a premature end to his career. Having fought on the royalist side he retired to his home, Newton-upon-Usk in Wales, to pursue a living as a physician. He published his most important volume of poems, *Silex Scintillans*, in 1650. He was not yet thirty. These poems were influenced by Herbert, but Vaughan added another dimension to the devotional manner he had forged: the optimism born out of spiritual transcendence. Some of his finest works discuss imaginative vision and the natural world with an eloquence not found again in English poetry until the Romantic period. In 'The Night' Vaughan describes Christ as

> So rare a flower,
> Within whose sacred leaves did lie
> The fullness of the deity. (ll. 16–18)

This is not purely aesthetic; it speaks of Christ's immanence throughout the natural world. For Vaughan, Christ is not one special flower but all flowers. In keeping with the hermetic philosophers whose work he knew, that immanence remains obscure until a moment of vision. So it is that the poet who appears at the beginning of 'Regeneration' sees 'high-spring' without but feels only 'frost within, / And surly winds'. The difference between that and Herbert's 'The Pilgrimage' (its immediate source) is that whereas Herbert is offered only the gloomy cave of Desperation and a wild of Passion, Vaughan is given a revelation:

> The unthrift sun shot vital gold
>   A thousand pieces,
> And heaven its azure did unfold
>   Chequered with snowy fleeces ... (ll. 41–4)

This is something new in poetry, purged of the weight of guilt and sin that overshadows Herbert. At the instant of regeneration Vaughan's body and mind, in harmony with the natural world, are transformed. Such energy is inherent within the natural world all the time, he argues, but only in exceptional moments can the flower be perceived beneath the 'sacred leaves' of outward being. It is consistent with this that in 'The Night' Vaughan emphasizes that Nicodemus found God not in the ostentation of temples with their rich ornaments, but in Christ himself, hidden and unseen at the dead of night.

Some of the best of his poems are driven by grief at the death of his younger brother William. But even then everything is turned into a kind of celebration. In 'They are all gone into the world of light!' (pp. 174–5) Vaughan uses the image of a star trapped in a cave to illustrate the idea of God within man, of life beyond death, and of the possibility of a return to a prelapsarian state. His preoccupation is with promise and potential – embodied in the images of the bud, the stone, the star and the crown.

Thomas Traherne shared with Vaughan an acute intensity of vision that lends his work a similar optimism. Traherne went so far as to reject the doctrine of original sin; instead he thought of sin as a habit acquired by contact with society – 'Shops, markets, taverns, coaches' and the 'Swearing and roaring boys' who inhabited them ('Eden', ll. 24–5). He was little regarded until the discovery of his poems in the early twentieth century aroused interest in him. Unhindered by notions of propriety (as he did not aim to publish his work), he is at liberty to write exactly what he believes – not unlike two later visionaries, Blake and Clare. It is clear from 'Innocence' that he regarded himself as like Adam, and thought the world was created entirely for his pleasure: 'I was an Adam there'. His view of his spiritual being sometimes places him on a par with God: 'all my mind was wholly every where' ('My Spirit', l. 57).

The period covered by this volume saw the Elizabethan age – one of relative stability – give way to one of violent turmoil. The resultant changes in the body politic would produce war-and postwar poetry that embodied the fears and hopes of those who lived through them. These works, and the great epic that would follow – *Paradise Lost* – sowed the seeds for the great poetry of the eighteenth and nineteenth centuries.

Further Reading

Corns, Thomas N. (ed.) (2001) *A Companion to Milton* (Oxford: Blackwell).

Cummings, Robert (ed.) (2000) *Seventeenth-Century Poetry: An Annotated Anthology* (Oxford: Blackwell).

Hattaway, Michael (ed.) (2001) *A Companion to English Renaissance Literature and Culture* (Oxford: Blackwell).

Kastan, David Scott (ed.) (1999) *A Companion to Shakespeare* (Oxford: Blackwell).

Lewalski, Barbara K. (2000) *The Life of John Milton* (Oxford: Blackwell).

Edmund Spenser
(?1552–1599)

Prothalamion: or, A Spousal Verse

Calm was the day, and through the trembling air
Sweet-breathing Zephyrus did softly play
A gentle spirit, that lightly did delay
Hot Titan's beams, which then did glister fair;
When I, (whom sullen care,   5
Through discontent of my long fruitless stay
In prince's court, and expectation vain
Of idle hopes, which still do fly away,
Like empty shadows, did afflict my brain,)
Walked forth to ease my pain   10
Along the shore of silver streaming Thames;
Whose rutty bank, the which his river hems,
Was painted all with variable flowers,
And all the meads adorned with dainty gems,
Fit to deck maidens' bowers,   15
And crown their paramours
Against the bridal day, which is not long:
    Sweet Thames! run softly, till I end my song.

There, in a meadow, by the river's side,
A flock of Nymphs I chanced to espy,   20
All lovely daughters of the flood thereby,
With goodly greenish locks, all loose untied,
As each had been a bride;
And each one had a little wicker basket,
Made of fine twigs, entrailed curiously,   25
In which they gathered flowers to fill their flasket,
And with fine fingers cropt full feateously
The tender stalks on high.
Of every sort, which in that meadow grew,
They gathered some; the violet, pallid blue,   30
The little daisy, that at evening closes,
The virgin lily, and the primrose true,

---

12 Rooty. 26 Vessel, basket. 27 Dexterously.

With store of vermeil roses,
To deck their bridegrooms' posies
Against the bridal day, which was not long:⁣   35
    Sweet Thames! run softly, till I end my song.

With that I saw two swans of goodly hue
Come softly swimming down along the lee;
Two fairer birds I yet did never see;
The snow, which doth the top of Pindus strew,   40
Did never whiter shew,
Nor Jove himself, when he a swan would be
For love of Leda, whiter did appear;
Yet Leda was (they say) as white as he,
Yet not so white as these, nor nothing near;   45
So purely white they were,
That even the gentle stream, the which them bare,
Seemed foul to them, and bade his billows spare
To wet their silken feathers, lest they might
Soil their fair plumes with water not so fair,   50
And mar their beauties bright,
That shone as heaven's light,
Against their bridal day, which was not long:
    Sweet Thames! run softly, till I end my song.

Eftsoons, the Nymphs, which now had flowers their fill,   55
Ran all in haste to see that silver brood,
As they came floating on the crystal flood;
Whom when they saw, they stood amazed still,
Their wondering eyes to fill;
Them seem'd they never saw a sight so fair,   60
Of fowls, so lovely, that they sure did deem
Them heavenly born, or to be that same pair
Which through the sky draw Venus' silver team;
For sure they did not seem
To be begot of any earthly seed,   65
But rather angels, or of angels' breed;
Yet were they bred of Somers-heat, they say,
In sweetest season, when each flower and weed
The earth did fresh array;
So fresh they seemed as day,   70
Even as their bridal day, which was not long:
    Sweet Thames! run softly, till I end my song.

Then forth they all out of their baskets drew
Great store of flowers, the honour of the field,

38 Stream.

That to the sense did fragrant odours yield,   75
All which upon those goodly birds they threw,
And all the waves did strew,
That like old Peneus' waters they did seem,
When down along by pleasant Tempe's shore,
Scattered with flowers, through Thessaly they stream,   80
That they appear, through lilies' plenteous store,
Like a bride's chamber floor.
Two of those Nymphs, meanwhile, two garlands bound
Of freshest flowers which in that mead they found,
The which presenting all in trim array,   85
Their snowy foreheads therewithal they crowned,
Whilst one did sing this lay,
Prepared against that day,
Against their bridal day, which was not long:
    Sweet Thames! run softly, till I end my song.   90

'Ye gentle Birds! the world's fair ornament,
And heaven's glory, whom this happy hour
Doth lead unto your lovers' blissful bower,
Joy may you have, and gentle hearts' content
Of your love's couplement;   95
And let fair Venus, that is Queen of Love,
With her heart-quelling son upon you smile,
Whose smile, they say, hath virtue to remove
All love's dislike, and friendship's faulty guile
For ever to assoil.   100
Let endless peace your steadfast hearts accord,
And blessed plenty wait upon your board;
And let your bed with pleasures chaste abound,
That fruitful issue may to you afford,
Which may your foes confound,   105
And make your joys redound
Upon your bridal day, which is not long:
    Sweet Thames! run softly, till I end my song.'

So ended she; and all the rest around
To her redoubled that her undersong,   110
Which said, their bridal day should not be long:
And gentle Echo from the neighbour ground
Their accents did resound.
So forth those joyous birds did pass along
Adown the lee, that to them murmured low,   115
As he would speak, but that he lacked a tongue,
Yet did by signs his glad affection show,
Making his stream run slow.

100 Remove.

And all the fowl which in his flood did dwell
Gan flock about these twain, that did excel   120
The rest, so far as Cynthia doth shend
The lesser stars. So they, enranged well,
Did on those two attend,
And their best service lend
Against their wedding day, which was not long: 125
   Sweet Thames! run softly, till I end my song.

At length they all to merry London came,
To merry London, my most kindly nurse,
That to me gave this life's first native source,
Though from another place I take my name,   130
An house of ancient fame:
There when they came, whereas those bricky towers
The which on Thames' broad aged back do ride,
Where now the studious lawyers have their bowers,
There whilome wont the Templar Knights to bide,   135
Till they decayed through pride;
Next whereunto there stands a stately place,
Where oft I gained gifts and goodly grace
Of that great lord, which therein wont to dwell,
Whose want too well now feels my friendless case;   140
But ah! here fits not well
Old woes, but joys, to tell
Against the bridal day, which is not long:
   Sweet Thames! run softly, till I end my song.

Yet therein now doth lodge a noble peer,   145
Great England's glory, and the world's wide wonder,
Whose dreadful name late through all Spain did thunder,
And Hercules' two pillars standing near
Did make to quake and fear:
Fair branch of honour, flower of chivalry!   150
That fillest England with thy triumph's fame,
Joy have thou of thy noble victory,
And endless happiness of thine own name
That promiseth the same;
That through thy prowess, and victorious arms,   155
Thy country may be freed from foreign harms,
And great Elisa's glorious name may ring
Through all the world, filled with thy wide alarms,
Which some brave Muse may sing
To ages following,   160
Upon the bridal day, which is not long:
   Sweet Thames! run softly, till I end my song.

121 Put to shame. **135** Formerly.

From those high towers this noble lord issuing,
Like radiant Hesper, when his golden hair
In the ocean billows he hath bathed fair,   165
Descended to the river's open viewing,
With a great train ensuing.
Above the rest were goodly to be seen
Two gentle Knights of lovely face and feature,
Beseeming well the bower of any queen,   170
With gifts of wit, and ornaments of nature,
Fit for so goodly stature,
That like the Twins of Jove they seem'd in sight,
Which deck the baldric of the heavens bright;
They two, forth pacing to the river's side,   175
Received those two fair Brides, their love's delight;
Which, at the appointed tide,
Each one did make his bride
Against their bridal day, which is not long:
    Sweet Thames! run softly, till I end my song.   180

From *The Faerie Queene*

1. The bower of Bliss (II. xii)

LXX

Eftsoons they heard a most melodious sound,
Of all that might delight a dainty ear,
Such as at once might not on living ground,
Save in this paradise, be heard elsewhere;   625
Right hard it was for wight which did it hear,
To read what manner music that might be;
For all that pleasing is to living ear
    Was there consorted in one harmony;
Birds, voices, instruments, winds, waters, all agree: 630

LXXI

The joyous birds, shrouded in cheerful shade,
Their notes unto the voice attempered sweet;
The angelical soft trembling voices made
To the instruments divine respondence meet;
The silver-sounding instruments did meet   635
With the base murmur of the waters' fall;
The waters' fall with difference discreet,
    Now soft, now loud, unto the wind did call;
The gentle warbling wind low answered to all.

174 Girdle.

LXXII

There, whence that music seemed heard to be,   640
Was the fair witch herself now solacing
With a new lover, whom, through sorcery
And witchcraft, she from far did thither bring:
There she had him now laid a slumbering
In secret shade after long wanton joys;   645
Whilst round about them pleasantly did sing
Many fair ladies and lascivious boys,
That ever mixt their song with light licentious toys.

LXXIII

And all that while right over him she hong
With her false eyes fast fixed in his sight,   650
As seeking medicine whence she was stong,
Or greedily depasturing delight;
And oft inclining down, with kisses light,
For fear of waking him, his lips bedewed,
And through his humid eyes did suck his sprite,   655
Quite molten into lust and pleasure lewd;
Wherewith she sighed soft, as if his case she rued.

LXXIV

The whiles some one did chaunt this lovely lay;
Ah! see, whoso fair thing dost fain to see,
In springing flower the image of thy day!   660
Ah! see the virgin rose, how sweetly she
Doth first peep forth with bashful modesty,
That fairer seems the less ye see her may!
Lo! see soon after how more bold and free
Her bared bosom she doth broad display,   665
Lo! see soon after how she fades and falls away!

LXXV

So passeth, in the passing of a day,
Of mortal life the leaf, the bud, the flower;
Ne more doth flourish after first decay,
That erst was sought to deck both bed and bower   670
Of many a lady, and many a paramour!
Gather therefore the rose whilst yet is prime,
For soon comes age that will her pride deflower:
Gather the rose of love whilst yet is time,
Whilst loving thou mayst loved be with equal crime   675

LXXVI

He ceased; and then gan all the choir of birds
Their diverse notes to attune unto his lay,
As in approvance of his pleasing words.

The constant pair heard all that he did say,
Yet swerved not, but kept their forward way   680
Through many covert groves and thickets close,
In which they creeping did at last display
That wanton Lady with her lover lose,
Whose sleepy head she in her lap did soft dispose.

LXXVII

Upon a bed of roses she was laid,   685
As faint through heat, or dight to pleasant sin;
And was arrayed, or rather disarrayed,
All in a veil of silk and silver thin,
That hid no whit her alabaster skin,
But rather showed more white, if more might be: 690
More subtle web Arachne cannot spin;
Nor the fine nets, which oft we woven see
Of scorched dew, do not in the air more lightly flee.

LXXVIII

Her snowy breast was bare to ready spoil
Of hungry eyes, which n'ote therewith be filled;   695
And yet through languor of her late sweet toil,
Few drops, more clear then nectar, forth distilled,
That like pure orient pearls adown it trilled;
And her fair eyes, sweet smiling in delight,
Moistened their fiery beams, with which she thrilled   700
Frail hearts, yet quenched not; like starry light,
Which, sparkling on the silent waves, does seem more bright.

LXXIX

The young man, sleeping by her, seemed to be
Some goodly swain of honourable place;
That certes it great pity was to see   705
Him his nobility so foul deface:
A sweet regard and amiable grace,
Mixed with manly sternness, did appear,
Yet sleeping, in his well-proportioned face
And on his tender lips the downy hair;   710
Did now but freshly spring, and silken blossoms bear.

LXXX

His warlike arms, the idle instruments
Of sleeping praise, were hung upon a tree;
And his brave shield, full of old moniments,
Was foully rased, that none the signs might see;   715
Ne for them, ne for honour cared he,

695 Could not.

Ne ought that did to his advancement tend;
But in lewd loves, and wasteful luxury,
His days, his goods, his body he did spend:
O horrible enchantment, that him so did blend!   720

LXXXI
The noble elfe and careful palmer drew
So nigh them, minding nought but lustful game,
That sudden forth they on them rushed, and threw
A subtle net, which only for that same
The skilful palmer formally did frame: 725
So held them under fast; the whiles the rest
Fled all away for fear of fouller shame.
The fair enchantress, so unwares opprest,
Tried all her arts and all her sleights thence out to wrest;

LXXXII
And eke her lover strove; but all in vain: 730
For that same net so cunningly was wound,
That neither guile nor force might it distrain.
They took them both, and both them strongly bound
In captive bands, which there they ready found:
But her in chains of adamant he tied;   735
For nothing else might keep her safe and sound:
But Verdant (so he hight) he soon untied,
And counsel sage in stead thereof to him applied.

LXXXIII
But all those pleasant bowers, and palace brave,
Guyon broke down with rigour pitiless: 740
Ne ought their goodly workmanship might save
Them from the tempest of his wrathfulness,
But that their bliss he turned to balefulness,
Their groves he felled; their gardens did deface;
Their arbours spoil; their cabinets suppress;   745
Their banquet-houses burn; their buildings race;
And, of the fairest late, now made the foullest place.

LXXXIV
Then led they her away, and eke that knight
They with them led, both sorrowful and said:
The way they came, the same returned they right,   750
Till they arrived where they lately had
Charmed those wild beasts that raged with fury mad;
Which, now awaking, fierce at them gan fly,

720 Blind. **725** Expressly. **732** Rend. **737** Was called. **745** Cottages. **746** Raze.

As in their mistress' rescue, whom they lad;
But them the palmer soon did pacify.   755
Then Guyon asked, what meant those beasts which there did lie.

LXXXV

Said he; 'These seeming beasts are men in deed,
Whom this enchantress hath transformed thus;
Whilome her lovers, which her lusts did feed,
Now turned into figures hideous,   760
According to their minds like monstruous.'
'Sad end,' quoth he, 'of life intemperate,
And mournful meed of joys delicious!
But, Palmer, if it might thee so aggrate,
Let them returned be unto their former state.'   765

LXXXVI

Straightway he with his virtuous staff them strook,
And straight of beasts they comely men became;
Yet being men they did unmanly look,
And stared ghastly; some for inward shame,
And some for wrath to see their captive Dame: 770
But one above the rest in special
That had an hog been late, hight Gryll by name,
Repined greatly, and did him miscall
That had from hoggish form him brought to natural.

LXXXVII

Said Guyon; 'See the mind of beastly man,   775
That hath so soon forgot the excellence
Of his creation, when he life began,
That now he chooseth with vile difference
To be a beast, and lack intelligence!'
To whom the Palmer thus; 'The dunghill kind   780
Delights in filth and foul incontinence:
Let Gryll be Gryll, and have his hoggish mind;
But let us hence depart whilst weather serves and wind.'

2. The garden of Adonis (III. vi)

XXX

In that same garden all the goodly flowers,
Wherewith dame Nature doth her beautify
And decks the garlands of her paramours,
Are fetched: there is the first seminary   265
Of all things that are born to live and die,

754 Led. 764 Please.

According to their kinds. Long work it were
Here to account the endless progeny
Of all the weeds that bud and blossom there;
But so much as doth need must needs be counted here.   270

XXXI

It sited was in fruitful soil of old,
And girt in with two walls on either side,
The one of iron, the other of bright gold,
That none might thorough break, nor overstride:
And double gates it had which opened wide,   275
By which both in and out men moten pass;
The one fair and fresh, the other old and dried:
Old Genius the porter of them was,
Old Genius, the which a double nature has.

XXXII

He letteth in, he letteth out to wend   280
All that to come into the world desire:
A thousand thousand naked babes attend
About him day and night, which do require
That he with fleshly weeds would them attire:
Such as him list, such as eternal fate   285
Ordained hath, he clothes with sinful mire,
And sendeth forth to live in mortal state,
Till they again return back by the hinder gate.

XXXIII

After that they again returned been,
They in that garden planted be again,   290
And grow afresh, as they had never seen
Fleshly corruption nor mortal pain:
Some thousand years so do they there remain,
And then of him are clad with other hue,
Or sent into the changeful world again,   295
Till thither they return where first they grew:
So, like a wheel, around they run from old to new.

XXXIV

Ne needs there gardener to set or sow,
To plant or prune; for of their own accord
All things, as they created were, do grow,   300
And yet remember well the mighty word
Which first was spoken by the Almighty Lord
That bade them to *increase and multiply:*
Ne do they need, with water of the ford

276 Might.

Or of the clouds, to moisten their roots dry;   305
For in themselves eternal moisture they imply.

XXXV

Infinite shapes of creatures there are bred,
And uncouth forms, which none yet ever knew:
And every sort is in a sundry bed
Set by itself, and ranked in comely row;   310
Some fit for reasonable souls to indue;
Some made for beasts, some made for birds to wear;
And all the fruitful spawn of fishes' hue
In endless ranks along enranged were,
That seemed the ocean could not contain them there.   315

XXXVI

Daily they grow, and daily forth are sent
Into the world, it to replenish more;
Yet is the stock not lessened nor spent,
But still remains in everlasting store
As it at first created was of yore: 320
For in the wide womb of the world there lies,
In hateful darkness and in deep horror,
An huge eternal Chaos, which supplies
The substances of Nature's fruitful progenies.

XXXVII

All things from thence do their first being fetch,   325
And borrow matter whereof they are made;
Which, whenas form and feature it does ketch,
Becomes a body, and doth then invade
The state of life out of the grisly shade.
That substance is eterne, and bideth so;   330
Ne, when the life decays and form does fade,
Doth it consume and into nothing go,
But changed is and often altered to and fro.

XXXVIII

The substance is not changed nor altered,
But the only form and outward fashion;   335
For every substance is conditioned
To change her hue, and sundry forms to don,
Meet for her temper and complexion:
For forms are variable, and decay
By course of kind and by occasion;   340
And that fair flower of beauty fades away,
As doth the lily fresh before the sunny ray.

306 Contain. **327** Obtain.

XXXIX

Great enemy to it, and to all the rest
That in the Garden of Adonis springs,
Is wicked Time; who with his scythe addrest   345
Does mow the flowering herbs and goodly things,
And all their glory to the ground down flings,
Where they do wither and are foully marred:
He flies about, and with his flaggy wings
Beats down both leaves and buds without regard,   350
Ne ever pity may relent his malice hard.

XL

Yet pity often did the gods relent,
To see so fair things marred and spiled quite:
And their great mother Venus did lament
The loss of her dear brood, her dear delight: 355
Her heart was pierced with pity at the sight,
When walking through the garden them she saw,
Yet no'te she find redress for such despite:
For all that lives is subject to that law:
All things decay in time, and to their end do draw.   360

XLI

But were it not that Time their troubler is,
All that in this delightful garden grows
Should happy be, and have immortal bliss:
For here all plenty and all pleasure flows;
And sweet Love gentle fits amongst them throws,   365
Without fell rancour or fond jealousy:
Frankly each paramour his leman knows;
Each bird his mate; ne any does envy
Their goodly merriment and gay felicity.

XLII

There is continual spring, and harvest there   370
Continual, both meeting at one time:
For both the boughs do laughing blossoms bear,
And with fresh colours deck the wanton prime,
And eke at once the heavy trees they climb,
Which seem to labour under their fruit's load: 375
The whiles the joyous birds make their pastime
Amongst the shady leaves, their sweet abode,
And their true loves without suspicion tell abroad.

XLIII

Right in the middest of that paradise
There stood a stately mount, on whose round top   380

358 Could not. **367** Mistress.

A gloomy grove of myrtle trees did rise,
Whose shady boughs sharp steel did never lop,
Nor wicked beasts their tender buds did crop,
But like a garland compassed the height,
And from their fruitful sides sweet gum did drop,   385
That all the ground, with precious dew bedight,
Threw forth most dainty odours and most sweet delight.

XLIV

And in the thickest covert of that shade
There was a pleasant arbour, not by art
But of the trees' own inclination made,   390
Which knitting their rank branches part to part,
With wanton ivy-twine entrayld athwart,
And eglantine and caprifole among,
Fashioned above within their inmost part,
That neither Phoebus' beams could through them throng,   395
Nor Aeolus' sharp blast could work them any wrong.

XLV

And all about grew every sort of flower,
To which sad lovers were transformed of yore;
Fresh Hyacinthus, Phoebus' paramour
And dearest love;   400
Foolish Narciss, that likes the watery shore;
Sad Amaranthus, made a flower but late,
Sad Amaranthus, in whose purple gore
Me seems I see Amintas' wretched fate,
To whom sweet poet's verse hath given endless date.   405

XLVI

There wont fair Venus often to enjoy
Her dear Adonis' joyous company,
And reap sweet pleasure of the wanton boy:
There yet, some say, in secret he does lie,
Lapped in flowers and precious spicery,   410
By her hid from the world, and from the skill
Of Stygian gods, which do her love envy;
But she herself, whenever that she will,
Possesseth him, and of his sweetness takes her fill:

XLVII

And sooth, it seems, they say; for he may not   415
For ever die, and ever buried be
In baleful night where all things are forgot;
All be he subject to mortality,

393 Woodbine. 418 Although.

Yet is eterne in mutability,
And by succession made perpetual,   420
Transformed oft, and changed diversly:
For him the father of all forms they call;
Therefore needs mote he live, that living gives to all.

XLVIII
There now he liveth in eternal bliss,
Joying his goddess, and of her enjoyed;   425
Ne feareth he henceforth that foe of his,
Which with his cruel tusk him deadly cloyed:
For that wild boar, the which him once annoyed,
She firmly hath imprisoned for aye
(That her sweet love his malice might avoid)   430
In a strong rocky cave, which is, they say,
Hewn underneath that mount, that none him loosen may.

XLIX
There now he lives in everlasting joy,
With many of the gods in company
Which thither haunt, and with the winged boy,   435
Sporting himself in safe felicity:
Who when he hath with spoils and cruelty
Ransacked the world, and in the woeful hearts
Of many wretches set his triumphs high,
Thither resorts, and, laying his sad darts   440
Aside, with fair Adonis plays his wanton parts.

L
And his true love, fair Psyche, with him plays,
Fair Psyche to him lately reconciled,
After long troubles and unmeet upbrays,
With which his mother Venus her reviled,   445
And eke himself her cruelly exiled:
But now in steadfast love and happy state
She with him lives, and hath him borne a child,
Pleasure, that doth both gods and men aggrate,
Pleasure, the daughter of Cupid and Psyche late.   450

3. Mutability claims to rule the world (VII. vii)

XIII
This great grandmother of all creatures bred,
Great Nature, ever young, yet full of eld;   110
Still moving, yet unmoved from her stead;

427 Pierced. **449** Charm.

Unseen of any, yet of all beheld;
Thus sitting in her throne, as I have teld,
Before her came Dame Mutability;
And, being low before her presence feld   115
With meek obeisance and humility,
Thus gan her plaintive plea with words to amplify:

XIV

'To thee, O greatest goddess, only great,
An humble suppliant lo! I lowly fly,
Seeking for right, which I of thee entreat;   120
Who right to all dost deal indifferently,
Damning all wrong and tortious injury,
Which any of thy creatures do to other,
Oppressing them with power unequally,
Sith of them all thou art the equal mother,   125
And knittest each to each, as brother unto brother:

XV

'To thee therefore of this same Jove I plain,
And of his fellow gods that feign to be,
That challenge to themselves the whole world's reign,
Of which the greatest part is due to me,   130
And heaven itself by heritage in fee:
For heaven and earth I both alike do deem,
Sith heaven and earth are both alike to thee;
And gods no more than men thou dost esteem:
For even the gods to thee, as men to gods, do seem.   135

XVI

'Then weigh, O sovereign goddess, by what right
These gods do claim the world's whole sovereignty;
And that is only due unto my might
Arrogate to themselves ambitiously:
As for the gods' own principality,   140
Which Jove usurps unjustly, that to be
My heritage, Jove's self cannot deny,
From my great grandsire Titan unto me
Derived by due descent; as is well known to thee.

XVII

'Yet mauger Jove, and all his gods beside,   145
I do possess the world's most regiment;
As if ye please it into parts divide,
And every part's inholders to convent

131 Property, possession. **145** In spite of. **146** Chief government. **147** Inhabitants. **147** Convene.

Shall to your eyes appear incontinent.
And first, the Earth (great mother of us all)   150
That only seems unmoved and permanent,
And unto Mutability not thrall,
Yet is she changed in part, and eke in general:

XVIII

'For all that from her springs, and is ybred,
However fair it flourish for a time,   155
Yet see we soon decay; and, being dead,
To turn again unto their earthly slime:
Yet, out of their decay and mortal crime,
We daily see new creatures to arise,
And of their winter spring another prime,   160
Unlike in form, and changed by strange disguise:
So turn they still about, and change in restless wise.

XIX

'As for her tenants; that is, man and beasts;
The beasts we daily see massacred die
As thralls and vassals unto men's beheasts;   165
And men themselves do change continually,
From youth to eld, from wealth to poverty,
From good to bad, from bad to worst of all:
Ne do their bodies only flit and fly;
But eke their minds (which they immortal call)   170
Still change and vary thoughts, as new occasions fall.

XX

'Ne is the water in more constant case;
Whether those same on high, or these below:
For the ocean moveth still from place to place;
And every river still doth ebb and flow;   175
Ne any lake, that seems most still and slow,
Ne pool so small, that can his smoothness hold
When any wind doth under heaven blow;
With which the clouds are also tossed and rolled,
Now like great hills; and straight, like sluices, them unfold.   180

XXI

'So likewise are all watry living wights
Still tossed and turned with continual change,
Never abiding in their steadfast plights:
The fish, still floating, do at random range,
And never rest, but evermore exchange   185
Their dwelling places, as the streams them carry:
Ne have the watry fowls a certain grange

149 Immediately. **167** Old age.

Wherein to rest, ne in one stead do tarry;
But flitting still do fly, and still their places vary.

XXII

'Next is the air: which who feels not by sense   190
(For of all sense it is the middle mean)
To flit still, and with subtle influence
Of his thin spirit all creatures to maintain
In state of life? O weak life! that does lean
On thing so tickle as the unsteady air,   195
Which every hour is changed, and altered clean
With every blast that bloweth foul or fair:
The fair doth it prolong; the foul doth it impair.

XXIII

'Therein the changes infinite behold,
Which to her creatures every minute chance;   200
Now boiling hot; straight freezing deadly cold;
Now fair sunshine, that makes all skip and dance;
Straight bitter storms, and baleful countenance
That makes them all to shiver and to shake:
Rain, hail, and snow do pay them sad penance,   205
And dreadful thunder-claps (that make them quake)
With flames and flashing lights that thousand changes make.

XXIV

'Last is the fire; which, though it live for ever,
Ne can be quenched quite; yet, every day,
We see his parts, so soon as they do sever,   210
To lose their heat and shortly to decay;
So makes himself his own consuming prey:
Ne any living creatures doth he breed;
But all, that are of others bred, doth slay;
And with their death his cruel life doth feed;   215
Nought leaving but their barren ashes without seed.

XXV

'Thus all these four (the which the groundwork be
Of all the world and of all living wights)
To thousand sorts of change we subject see:
Yet are they changed by other wondrous sleights   220
Into themselves, and lose their native mights;
The fire to air, and the air to water sheer,
And water into earth; yet water fights
With fire, and air with earth, approaching near;
Yet all are in one body, and as one appear.   225

195 Uncertain.

XXVI

'So in them all reigns Mutability;
However these, that gods themselves do call,
Of them do claim the rule and sovereignty;
As Vesta, of the fire ethereal;
Vulcan of this with us so usual;   230
Ops, of the earth; and Juno, of the air;
Neptune, of seas; and Nymphs, of rivers all:
   For all those rivers to me subject are;
And all the rest, which they usurp, be all my share.

XXVII

'Which to approven true, as I have told,   235
Vouchsafe, O goddess, to thy presence call
The rest which do the world in being hold;
As times and seasons of the year that fall:
Of all the which demand in general,
Or judge thyself, by verdict of thine eye,   240
Whether to me they are not subject all.'
   Nature did yield thereto; and by-and-by
Bade Order call them all before her Majesty.

XXVIII

So forth issued the Seasons of the year:
First, lusty Spring all dight in leaves of flowers,   245
That freshly budded and new blooms did bear,
In which a thousand birds had built their bowers
That sweetly sung to call forth paramours;
And in his hand a javelin he did bear,
And on his head (as fit for warlike stoures)   250
A gilt engraven morion he did wear;
   That as some did him love, so others did him fear.

XXIX

Then came the jolly Summer, being dight
In a thin silken cassock coloured green,
That was unlined all, to be more light: 255
And on his head a garland well beseen
He wore, from which as he had chafed been
The sweat did drop; and in his hand he bore
A bow and shafts, as he in forest green
Had hunted late the leopard or the boar,   260
   And now would bathe his limbs with labour heated sore.

XXX

Then came the Autumn all in yellow clad,
As though he joyed in his plenteous store,

250 Encounters.

Laden with fruits that made him laugh, full glad
That he had banished hunger, which before   265
Had by the belly oft him pinched sore:
Upon his head a wreath, that was enrolled
With ears of corn of every sort, he bore;
And in his hand a sickle he did hold,
To reap the ripened fruits the which the earth had yold.   270

XXXI

Lastly, came Winter clothed all in frieze,
Chattering his teeth for cold that did him chill;
Whilst on his hoary beard his breath did freeze,
And the dull drops, that from his purpled bill
As from a limbec did adown distill: 275
In his right hand a tipped staff he held,
With which his feeble steps he stayed still;
For he was faint with cold, and weak with eld;
That scarce his loosed limbs he able was to weld.

XXXII

These, marching softly, thus in order went.   280
And after them the Months all riding came:
First, sturdy March, with brows full sternly bent
And armed strongly, rode upon a ram,
The same which over Hellespontus swam;
Yet in his hand a spade he also hent,   285
And in a bag all sorts of seeds ysame,
Which on the earth he strewed as he went,
And filled her womb with fruitful hope of nourishment.

XXXIII

Next came fresh April, full of lustyhed,
And wanton as a kid whose horn new buds: 290
Upon a bull he rode, the same which led
Europa floating through the Argolic floods;
His horns were gilden all with golden studs,
And garnished with garlands goodly dight
Of all the fairest flowers and freshest buds   295
Which the earth brings forth; and wet he seemed in sight
With waves, through which he waded for his love's delight.

XXXIV

Then came fair May, the fairest maid on ground,
Decked all with dainties of her season's pride,
And throwing flowers out of her lap around: 300
Upon two brethren's shoulders she did ride,
The Twins of Leda; which on either side
Supported her like to their sovereign queen:

Lord! how all creatures laughed when her they spied,
And leaped and danced as they had ravished been!   305
And Cupid self about her fluttered all in green.

XXXV

And after her came jolly June, arrayed
All in green leaves, as he a player were;
Yet in his time he wrought as well as played,
That by his plough-irons might right well appear: 310
Upon a crab he rode, that him did bear
With crooked crawling steps an uncouth pace,
And backward yode, as bargemen wont to fare
Bending their force contrary to their face;
Like that ungracious crew which feigns demurest grace   315

XXXVI

Then came hot July boiling like to fire,
That all his garments he did cast away:
Upon a lion raging yet with ire
He boldly rode, and made him to obey:
(It was the beast that whilome did foray   320
The Nemaean forest, till the Amphytrionide
Him slew, and with his hide did him array)
Behind his back a scythe, and by his side
Under his belt he bore a sickle circling wide.

XXXVII

The sixth was August, being rich arrayed   325
In garment all of gold down to the ground:
Yet rode he not, but led a lovely maid
Forth by the lily hand, the which was crowned
With ears of corn, and full her hand was found:
That was the righteous Virgin, which of old   330
Lived here on earth, and plenty made abound;
But, after wrong was loved, and justice sold,
She left the unrighteous world, and was to heaven extolled.

XXXVIII

Next him September marched eke on foot;
Yet was he heavy laden with the spoil   335
Of harvest's riches, which he made his boot,
And him enriched with bounty of the soil:
In his one hand, as fit for harvest's toil,
He held a knife-hook; and in the other hand
A Pair of Weights, with which he did assoil   340
Both more and less, where it in doubt did stand,
And equal gave to each as Justice duly scanned.

313 Went. **330** Astraea. **340** Determine.

XXXIX

Then came October full of merry glee;
For yet his noule was totty of the must,
Which he was treading in the wine-vats' see,   345
And of the joyous oil, whose gentle gust
Made him so frolic and so full of lust:
Upon a dreadful scorpion he did ride,
The same which by Diana's doom unjust
Slew great Orion; and eke by his side   350
He had his ploughing-share and coulter ready tied.

XL

Next was November; he full gross and fat
As fed with lard, and that right well might seem;
For he had been a fatting hogs of late,
That yet his brows with sweat did reek and steam,   355
And yet the season was full sharp and breem;
In planting eke he took no small delight:
Whereon he rode, not easy was to deem;
For it a dreadful centaur was in sight,
The seed of Saturn and fair Nais, Chiron hight.   360

XLI

And after him came next the chill December:
Yet he, through merry feasting which he made
And great bonfires, did not the cold remember;
His Saviour's birth his mind so much did glad:
Upon a shaggy-bearded goat he rode,   365
The same wherewith Dan Jove in tender years,
They say, was nourished by the Idaean maid;
And in his hand a broad deep bowl he bears,
Of which he freely drinks an health to all his peers.

XLII

Then came old January, wrapped well   370
In many weeds to keep the cold away;
Yet did he quake and quiver like to quell,
And blow his nails to warm them if he may;
For they were numbed with holding all the day
An hatchet keen, with which he felled wood   375
And from the trees did lop the needless spray:
Upon an huge great earth-pot stone he stood,
From whose wide mouth there flowed forth the Roman Flood.

XLIII

And lastly came cold February, sitting
In an old waggon, for he could not ride,   380

344 Head. 344 Dizzy. 344 New wine. 356 Piercing. 372 Perish.

Drawn of two Fishes for the season fitting,
Which through the flood before did softly slide
And swim away; yet had he by his side
His plough and harness fit to till the ground,
And tools to prune the trees, before the pride   385
Of hasting prime did make them burgeon round,
So passed the twelve months forth, and their due places found.

XLIV

And after these there came the day and night,
Riding together both with equal pace;
The one on a palfrey black, the other white: 390
But night had covered her uncomely face
With a black veil, and held in hand a mace,
On top whereof the moon and stars were pight,
And sleep and darkness round about did trace:
But day did bear upon his sceptre's height   395
The goodly sun encompassed all with beames bright.

XLV

Then came the Hours, fair daughters of high Jove
And timely night; the which were all endued
With wondrous beauty fit to kindle love;
But they were virgins all, and love eschewed   400
That might forslack the charge to them foreshowed
By mighty Jove; who did them porters make
Of heaven's gate (whence all the gods issued)
Which they did daily watch, and nightly wake
By even turns, ne ever did their charge forsake.   405

XLVI

And after all came Life; and lastly Death:
Death with most grim and grisly visage seen,
Yet is he nought but parting of the breath;
Ne ought to see, but like a shade to ween,
Unbodied, unsouled, unheard, unseen: 410
But Life was like a fair young lusty boy,
Such as they feign Dan Cupid to have been,
Full of delightful health and lively joy,
Decked all with flowers and wings of gold fit to employ.

XLVII

When these were past, thus gan the Titaness;   415
'Lo! mighty Mother, now be judge, and say
Whether in all thy creatures more or less
CHANGE doth not reign and bear the greatest sway:

393 Placed. **401** Cause, neglect. **401** Previously intrusted.

For who sees not that Time on all doth prey?
But times do change and move continually: 420
So nothing here long standeth in one stay:
Wherefore this lower world who can deny
But to be subject still to Mutability?'

Sir Walter Ralegh
(?1552–1618)

The Nymph's Reply to the Shepherd

If all the world and love were young,
And truth in every shepherd's tongue,
These pretty pleasures might me move
To live with thee and be thy love.

Time drives the flocks from field to fold,　　　　　5
When rivers rage and rocks grow cold,
And Philomel becometh dumb,
The rest complains of cares to come.

The flowers do fade, and wanton fields
To wayward winter reckoning yields,　　　　　10
A honey tongue, a heart of gall,
Is fancy's spring, but sorrow's fall.

Thy gowns, thy shoes, thy beds of roses,
Thy cap, thy kirtle, and thy posies,
Soon break, soon wither, soon forgotten:　　　　　15
In folly ripe, in reason rotten.

Thy belt of straw and ivy buds,
Thy coral clasps and amber studs,
All these in me no means can move
To come to thee, and be thy love.　　　　　20

But could youth last, and love still breed,
Had joys no date, nor age no need,
Then these delights my mind might move
To live with thee, and be thy love.

Fulke Greville, Lord Brooke (1554–1628)

From *Caelica*

Sonnet 69

When all this All doth pass from age to age,
And revolution in a circle turn,
Then heavenly justice doth appear like rage,
The caves do roar, the very seas do burn,
    Glory grows dark, the sun becomes a night,   5
    And makes this great world feel a greater might.

When Love doth change his seat from heart to heart,
And Worth about the wheel of fortune goes,
Grace is diseased, Desert seems overthwart,
Vows are forlorn, and Truth doth credit lose,   10
    Chance then gives law, Desire must be wise,
    And look more ways than one, or lose her eyes.

My age of joy is past, of woe begun,
Absence my presence is, strangeness my grace,
With them that walk against me, is my sun: 15
The wheel is turned, I hold the lowest place,
    What can be good to me since my love is
    To do me harm, content to do amiss?

Sonnet 86

The earth with thunder torn, with fire blasted,
With waters drowned, with windy palsy shaken
Cannot for this with heaven be distasted,
Since thunder, rain and winds from earth are taken:
Man torn with love, with inward furies blasted,   5
Drowned with despair, with fleshly lustings shaken,
Cannot for this with heaven be distasted,
Love, fury, lustings out of man are taken.

Then man, endure thy self, those clouds will vanish;
Life is a top which whipping sorrow driveth;   10
Wisdom must bear what our flesh cannot banish,

The humble lead, the stubborn bootless striveth:
Or man, forsake thyself, to heaven turn thee,
Her flames enlighten nature, never burn thee.

Sonnet 99

Down in the depth of mine iniquity,
That ugly centre of infernal spirits;
Where each sin feels her own deformity
In these peculiar torments she inherits,
    Deprived of human graces, and divine,   5
      Even there appears this saving God of mine.

And in this fatal mirror of transgression,
Shows man as fruit of his degeneration,
The error's ugly infinite impression
Which bears the faithless down to desperation,   10
    Deprived of human graces, and divine,
      Even there appears this saving God of mine.

In power and truth, Almighty and eternal,
Which on the sin reflects strange desolation,
With glory scourging all the spirits infernal,   15
And uncreated hell with unprivation;
    Deprived of human graces, not divine,
      Even there appears this saving God of mine.

For on this spiritual cross condemned lying
To pains infernal by eternal doom   20
I see my Saviour for the same sins dying
And, from that hell I feared, to free me come;
    Deprived of human graces, not divine,
      Thus hath his death raised up this soul of mine.

Sonnet 100

In night when colours all to black are cast,
Distinction lost, or gone down with the light;
The eye a watch to inward senses placed,
Not seeing, yet still having power of sight,

Gives vain alarums to the inward sense,   5
Where fear stirred up with witty tyranny,
Confounds all powers, and thorough self-offence,
Doth forge and raise impossibility:

Such as in thick depriving darknesses,
Proper reflections of the error be,   10

And images of self-confusednesses,
Which hurt imaginations only see;
   And from this nothing seen, tells news of devils,
   Which but expressions be of inward evils.

Sir Philip Sidney
(1554–1586)

From *Certain Sonnets*

Sonnet 31

Thou blind man's mark, thou fool's self-chosen snare,
Fond fancy's scum, and dregs of scattered thought;
Band of all evils, cradle of causeless care;
Thou web of will, whose end is never wrought;
Desire, desire! I have too dearly bought,   5
With price of mangled mind, thy worthless ware;
Too long, too long, asleep thou hast me brought,
Who should my mind to higher things prepare.
But yet in vain thou hast my ruin sought;
In vain thou madest me to vain things aspire;   10
In vain thou kindlest all thy smoky fire;
For virtue hath this better lesson taught,–
Within myself to seek my only hire,
Desiring nought but how to kill desire.

Sonnet 32

Leave me, O love which reachest but to dust;
And thou, my mind, aspire to higher things;
Grow rich in that which never taketh rust,
Whatever fades but fading pleasure brings.
Draw in thy beams, and humble all thy might   5
To that sweet yoke where lasting freedoms be;
Which breaks the clouds and opens forth the light,
That doth both shine and give us sight to see.
O take fast hold; let that light be thy guide
In this small course which birth draws out to death,   10
And think how evil becometh him to slide,
Who seeketh heav'n, and comes of heav'nly breath.
    Then farewell, world; thy uttermost I see;
    Eternal love, maintain thy life in me.

Splendidis longum valedico nugis.

From *Astrophil and Stella*

Sonnet 1

Loving in truth, and fain in verse my love to show,
   That she, dear she, might take some pleasure of my pain,
   Pleasure might cause her read, reading might make her know,
   Knowledge might pity win, and pity grace obtain –
I sought fit words to paint the blackest face of woe;   5
   Studying inventions fine, her wits to entertain,
   Oft turning others' leaves to see if thence would flow
   Some fresh and fruitful showers upon my sun-burned brain.
But words came halting forth, wanting invention's stay;
   Invention, nature's child, fled step-dame Study's blows,   10
   And others' feet still seemed but strangers in my way.
Thus, great with child to speak, and helpless in my throes,
   Biting my truant pen, beating myself for spite,
   Fool, said my muse to me, look in thy heart and write.

Sonnet 27

Because I oft, in dark abstracted guise,
   Seem most alone in greatest company,
   With dearth of words, or answers quite awry,
To them that would make speech of speech arise,
They deem, and of that doom the rumour flies,   5
   That poison foul of bubbling pride doth lie
   So in my swelling breast, that only I
Fawn on myself, and others do despise.
   Yet pride, I think, doth not my soul possess,
Which looks too oft in his unflattering glass;   10
But one worse fault, ambition, I confess,
That makes me oft my best friends overpass,
   Unseen, unheard, while thought to highest place
   Bends all his powers, even unto Stella's grace.

Sonnet 31

With how sad steps, O moon, thou climb'st the skies!
   How silently, and with how wan a face!
   What! may it be that even in heav'nly place
   That busy archer his sharp arrows tries?
Sure, if that long-with-love-acquainted eyes   5
   Can judge of love, thou feel'st a lover's case;
   I read it in thy looks–thy languished grace
   To me, that feel the like, thy state descries.
Then, even of fellowship, O moon, tell me,

Is constant love deemed there but want of wit?   10
   Are beauties there as proud as here they be?
Do they above love to be loved, and yet
   Those lovers scorn whom that love doth possess?
   Do they call virtue there ungratefulness?

Sonnet 34

Come, let me write. And to what end? To ease
   A burthened heart. How can words ease, which are
   The glasses of thy daily vexing care?
   Oft cruel fights well pictured forth do please.
Art not ashamed to publish thy disease?   5
   Nay, that may breed my fame, it is so rare.
   But will not wise men think thy words fond ware?
   Then be they close, and so none shall displease.
What idler thing than speak and not be heard?
   What harder thing than smart and not to speak?   10
   Peace, foolish wit! with wit my wit is marred.
Thus write I, while I doubt to write, and wreak
   My harms on ink's poor loss. Perhaps some find
   Stella's great powers, that so confuse my mind.

Sonnet 39

Come sleep! O sleep, the certain knot of peace,
   The baiting place of wit, the balm of woe,
   The poor man's wealth, the prisoner's release,
   The indifferent judge between the high and low;
With shield of proof shield me from out the prease   5
   Of those fierce darts despair at me doth throw;
   O make in me those civil wars to cease;
   I will good tribute pay, if thou do so.
Take thou of me smooth pillows, sweetest bed,
   A chamber deaf to noise and blind to light,   10
   A rosy garland and a weary head;
And if these things, as being thine by right,
   Move not thy heavy grace, thou shalt in me,
   Livelier than elsewhere, Stella's image see.

Sonnet 45

Stella oft sees the very face of woe
   Painted in my beclouded stormy face,
   But cannot skill to pity my disgrace,
   Not though thereof the cause herself she know;
Yet hearing late a fable, which did show   5
   Of lovers never known a grievous case,

Pity thereof gat in her breast such place
   That, from the sea derived, tears' spring did flow.
Alas, if fancy, drawn by imaged things
   Though false, yet with free scope, more grace doth breed   10
   Than servant's wrack, where new doubts honour brings;
Then think, my dear, that you in me do read
   Of lovers' ruin some sad tragedy.
   I am not I; pity the tale of me.

Sonnet 54

Because I breathe not love to every one,
   Nor do not use set colours for to wear,
   Nor nourish special locks of vowed hair,
   Nor give each speech a full point of a groan,
The courtly nymphs, acquainted with the moan   5
   Of them who in their lips Love's standard bear,
   What, he! say they of me, Now I dare swear
   He cannot love; no, no, let him alone.
And think so still, so Stella know my mind;
   Profess indeed I do not Cupid's art;   10
   But you, fair maids, at length this true shall find,
That his right badge is but worn in the heart;
   Dumb swans, not chatt'ring pies, do lovers prove;
   They love indeed who quake to say they love.

Sonnet 94

Grief find the words, for thou hast made my brain
   So dark with misty vapours which arise
   From out thy heavy mould, that inbent eyes
Can scarce discern the shape of mine own pain.
Do thou then (for thou canst), do thou complain   5
   For my poor soul which now that sickness tries,
   Which even to sense, sense of itself denies,
Though harbingers of death lodge there his train.
   Or if thy love of plaint yet mine forbears,
As of a caitiff not vouchsafed to die,   10
Yet wail thyself, and wail with causeful tears,
That though in wretchedness thy life doth lie,
Yet grow'st more wretched than thy nature bears,
By being placed in such a wretch as I.

Michael Drayton
(1563–1631)

From *Idea*

Sonnet 6

How many paltry, foolish, painted things,
That now in coaches trouble every street,
Shall be forgotten, whom no poet sings,
Ere they be well wrapped in their winding sheet!
   Where I to thee eternity shall give,   5
When nothing else remaineth of these days,
And queens hereafter shall be glad to live
Upon the alms of thy superfluous praise;
   Virgins and matrons reading these my rhymes,
Shall be so much delighted with thy story,   10
That they shall grieve they lived not in these times,
To have seen thee, their sex's only glory.
   So shalt thou fly above the vulgar throng,
   Still to survive in my immortal song.

Sonnet 13

You're not alone when you are still alone;
O God! from you that I could private be!
Since you one were, I never since was one;
Since you in me, myself since out of me.
   Transported from myself into your being,   5
Though either distant, present yet to either;
Senseless with too much joy, each other seeing;
And only absent when we are together.
   Give me my self, and take your self again!
Devise some means but how I may forsake you!   10
So much is mine that doth with you remain,
That taking what is mine, with me I take you.
   You do bewitch me! O that I could fly
   From my self you, or from your own self I!

Christopher Marlowe
(1564–1593)

The Passionate Shepherd to his Love

Come live with me and be my love,
And we will all the pleasures prove
That valleys, groves, hills, and fields,
Woods, or steepy mountain yields.

And we will sit upon the rocks,   5
Seeing the shepherds feed their flocks,
By shallow rivers to whose falls
Melodious birds sings madrigals.

And I will make thee beds of roses
And a thousand fragrant posies,   10
A cap of flowers, and a kirtle
Embroidered all with leaves of myrtle;

A gown made of the finest wool
Which from our pretty lambs we pull;
Fair lined slippers for the cold,   15
With buckles of the purest gold;

A belt of straw and ivy buds,
With coral clasps and amber studs:
And if these pleasures may thee move,
Come live with me, and be my love.   20

The shepherds' swains shall dance and sing
For thy delight each May morning:
If these delights thy mind may move,
Then live with me and be my love.

William Shakespeare
(1564–1616)

From *Sonnets*

Sonnet 1

From fairest creatures we desire increase,
  That thereby beauty's rose might never die,
But as the riper should by time decease,
  His tender heir might bear his memory:
But thou, contracted to thine own bright eyes,   5
  Feed'st thy light's flame with self-substantial fuel,
Making a famine where abundance lies,
  Thyself thy foe, to thy sweet self too cruel.
Thou that art now the world's fresh ornament,
  And only herald to the gaudy spring,   10
Within thine own bud buriest thy content,
  And, tender churl, mak'st waste in niggarding.
Pity the world, or else this glutton be,
To eat the world's due, by the grave and thee.

Sonnet 2

When forty winters shall besiege thy brow,
  And dig deep trenches in thy beauty's field,
Thy youth's proud livery, so gazed on now,
  Will be a tattered weed, of small worth held:
Then being asked where all thy beauty lies,   5
  Where all the treasure of thy lusty days;
To say, within thine own deep sunken eyes,
  Were an all-eating shame, and thriftless praise.
How much more praise deserved thy beauty's use,
  If thou couldst answer – 'This fair child of mine   10
Shall sum my count, and make my old excuse'–
  Proving his beauty by succession thine!
This were to be new-made when thou art old,
And see thy blood warm when thou feel'st it cold.

Sonnet 12

When I do count the clock that tells the time,
  And see the brave day sunk in hideous night;
When I behold the violet past prime,
  And sable curls, all silvered o'er with white;
When lofty trees I see barren of leaves,   5
  Which erst from heat did canopy the herd,
And summer's green all girded up in sheaves,
  Borne on the bier with white and bristly beard;
Then of thy beauty do I question make,
  That thou among the wastes of time must go,   10
Since sweets and beauties do themselves forsake,
  And die as fast as they see others grow;
And nothing 'gainst Time's scythe can make defence,
Save breed, to brave him when he takes thee hence.

Sonnet 18

Shall I compare thee to a summer's day?
  Thou art more lovely and more temperate:
Rough winds do shake the darling buds of May,
  And summer's lease hath all too short a date:
Sometime too hot the eye of heaven shines,   5
  And often is his gold complexion dimmed;
And every fair from fair sometime declines,
  By chance, or nature's changing course, untrimmed;
But thy eternal summer shall not fade,
  Nor lose possession of that fair thou owest;   10
Nor shall Death brag thou wander'st in his shade,
  When in eternal lines to time thou growest;
So long as men can breathe, or eyes can see,
So long lives this, and this gives life to thee.

Sonnet 29

When in disgrace with fortune and men's eyes,
  I all alone beweep my outcast state,
And trouble deaf heaven with my bootless cries,
  And look upon myself, and curse my fate,
Wishing me like to one more rich in hope,   5
  Featured like him, like him with friends possessed,
Desiring this man's art, and that man's scope,
  With what I most enjoy contented least;
Yet in these thoughts myself almost despising,
  Haply I think on thee, – and then my state   10
(Like to the lark at break of day arising

From sullen earth) sings hymns at heaven's gate;
For thy sweet love remembered, such wealth brings,
That then I scorn to change my state with kings.

Sonnet 30

When to the sessions of sweet silent thought
  I summon up remembrance of things past,
I sigh the lack of many a thing I sought,
  And with old woes new wail my dear time's waste:
Then can I drown an eye, unused to flow,   5
  For precious friends hid in death's dateless night,
And weep afresh love's long since cancelled woe,
  And moan the expense of many a vanished sight.
Then can I grieve at grievances foregone,
  And heavily from woe to woe tell o'er   10
The sad account of fore-bemoaned moan,
  Which I new pay as if not paid before.
But if the while I think on thee, dear friend,
All losses are restored, and sorrows end.

Sonnet 55

Not marble, not the gilded monuments
  Of princes, shall outlive this powerful rhyme;
But you shall shine more bright in these contents
  Than unswept stone, besmeared with sluttish time.
When wasteful war shall statues overturn,   5
  And broils root out the work of masonry,
Nor Mars his sword nor war's quick fire shall burn
  The living record of your memory.
'Gainst death and all-oblivious enmity
  Shall you pace forth; your praise shall still find room,   10
Even in the eyes of all posterity
  That wear this world out to the ending doom.
So, till the judgment that yourself arise,
You live in this, and dwell in lovers' eyes.

Sonnet 60

Like as the waves make towards the pebbled shore,
  So do our minutes hasten to their end;
Each changing place with that which goes before,
  In sequent toil all forwards do contend.
Nativity, once in the main of light,   5
  Crawls to maturity, wherewith being crowned,
Crooked eclipses 'gainst his glory fight,
  And Time that gave doth now his gift confound.

Time doth transfix the flourish set on youth,
   And delves the parallels in beauty's brow;   10
Feeds on the rarities of nature's truth,
   And nothing stands but for his scythe to mow.
And yet to times in hope my verse shall stand,
Praising thy worth, despite his cruel hand.

Sonnet 64

When I have seen by Time's fell hand defaced
   The rich proud cost of outworn buried age;
When sometime lofty towers I see down-rased,
   And brass eternal slave to mortal rage;
When I have seen the hungry ocean gain   5
   Advantage on the kingdom of the shore,
And the firm soil win of the wat'ry main,
   Increasing store with loss, and loss with store;
When I have seen such interchange of state,
   Or state itself confounded to decay,   10
Ruin hath taught me thus to ruminate
   That time will come and take my love away.
This thought is as a death, which cannot choose
But weep to have that which it fears to lose.

Sonnet 71

No longer mourn for me when I am dead,
   Than you shall hear the surly sullen bell
Give warning to the world that I am fled
   From this vile world, with vilest worms to dwell:
Nay, if you read this line, remember not   5
   The hand that writ it, for I love you so,
That I in your sweet thoughts would be forgot,
   If thinking on me then should make you woe.
Oh if (I say) you look upon this verse,
   When I perhaps compounded am with clay,   10
Do not so much as my poor name rehearse,
   But let your love even with my life decay:
Lest the wise world should look into your moan,
And mock you with me after I am gone.

Sonnet 73

That time of year thou mayst in me behold
   When yellow leaves, or none, or few, do hang
Upon those boughs which shake against the cold,
   Bare ruined choirs, where late the sweet birds sang.
In me thou seest the twilight of such day   5
   As after sunset fadeth in the west,

Which by and by black night doth take away,
　　Death's second self, that seals up all in rest.
In me thou seest the glowing of such fire,
　　That on the ashes of his youth doth lie,　　　　　　　　10
As the death-bed whereon it must expire,
　　Consumed with that which it was nourished by.
This thou perceiv'st, which makes thy love more strong,
To love that well which thou must leave ere long:

Sonnet 90

Then hate me when thou wilt; if ever, now;
　　Now while the world is bent my deeds to cross,
Join with the spite of fortune, make me bow,
　　And do not drop in for an after-loss:
Ah, do not, when my heart hath scaped this sorrow,　　　　5
　　Come in the rearward of a conquered woe;
Give not a windy night a rainy morrow,
　　To linger out a purposed overthrow.
If thou wilt leave me, do not leave me last,
　　When other petty griefs have done their spite,　　　　10
But in the onset come; so shall I taste
　　At first the very worst of fortune's might;
And other strains of woe, which now seem woe,
Compared with loss of thee will not seem so.

Sonnet 91

Some glory in their birth, some in their skill,
　　Some in their wealth, some in their body's force;
Some in their garments, though newfangled ill;
　　Some in their hawks and hounds, some in their horse;
And every humour hath his adjunct pleasure,　　　　　　5
　　Wherein it finds a joy above the rest;
But these particulars are not my measure,
　　All these I better in one general best.
Thy love is better than high birth to me,
　　Richer than wealth, prouder than garments' cost,　　　10
Of more delight than hawks or horses be;
　　And, having thee, of all men's pride I boast.
Wretched in this alone, that thou mayst take
All this away, and me most wretched make.

Sonnet 94

They that have power to hurt and will do none,
　　That do not do the thing they most do show,
Who, moving others, are themselves as stone,
　　Unmoved, cold, and to temptation slow;

They rightly do inherit heaven's graces,   5
  And husband nature's riches from expense;
They are the lords and owners of their faces,
  Others but stewards of their excellence.
The summer's flower is to the summer sweet,
  Though to itself it only live and die;   10
But if that flower with base infection meet,
  The basest weed outbraves his dignity:
For sweetest things turn sourest by their deeds;
Lilies that fester smell far worse than weeds.

Sonnet 110

Alas, 'tis true, I have gone here and there,
  And made myself a motley to the view,
Gored mine own thoughts, sold cheap what is most dear,
  Made old offences of affections new.
Most true it is, that I have look'd on truth   5
  Askance and strangely; but, by all above,
These blenches gave my heart another youth,
  And worse essays proved thee my best of love.
Now all is done, have what shall have no end:
  Mine appetite I never more will grind   10
On newer proof, to try an older friend,
  A god in love, to whom I am confined.
Then give me welcome, next my heaven the best,
Even to thy pure and most most loving breast.

Sonnet 115

Those lines that I before have writ, do lie,
  Even those that said I could not love you dearer;
Yet then my judgment knew no reason why
  My most full flame should afterwards burn clearer.
But reckoning time, whose millioned accidents   5
  Creep in 'twixt vows, and change decrees of kings,
Tan sacred beauty, blunt the sharp'st intents,
  Divert strong minds to the course of altering things;
Alas, why, fearing of Time's tyranny,
  Might I not then say, 'Now I love you best',   10
When I was certain o'er incertainty,
  Crowning the present, doubting of the rest?
Love is a babe; then might I not say so,
To give full growth to that which still doth grow?

Sonnet 116

Let me not to the marriage of true minds
  Admit impediments; love is not love

Which alters when it alteration finds,
　Or bends with the remover to remove.
Oh no, it is an ever-fixed mark, 5
　That looks on tempests and is never shaken;
It is the star to every wandering bark,
　Whose worth's unknown, although his height be taken.
Love's not Time's fool, though rosy lips and cheeks
　Within his bending sickle's compass come; 10
Love alters not with his brief hours and weeks,
　But bears it out even to the edge of doom.
If this be error, and upon me proved,
I never writ, nor no man ever loved.

Sonnet 121

'Tis better to be vile than vile esteemed,
　When not to be receives reproach of being,
And the just pleasure lost, which is so deemed
　Not by our feeling, but by others' seeing.
For why should others' false adulterate eyes 5
　Give salutation to my sportive blood?
Or on my frailties why are frailer spies,
　Which in their wills count bad what I think good?
No, I am that I am; and they that level
　At my abuses, reckon up their own: 10
I may be straight, though they themselves be bevel;
　By their rank thoughts my deeds must not be shown,
Unless this general evil they maintain–
All men are bad and in their badness reign.

Sonnet 129

The expense of spirit in a waste of shame
　Is lust in action; and till action, lust
Is perjured, murderous, bloody, full of blame,
　Savage, extreme, rude, cruel, not to trust;
Enjoyed no sooner, but despised straight; 5
　Past reason hunted; and no sooner had,
Past reason hated, as a swallowed bait,
　On purpose laid to make the taker mad:
Mad in pursuit, and in possession so;
　Had, having, and in quest to have, extreme; 10
A bliss in proof – and proved, a very woe;
　Before, a joy proposed; behind, a dream;
All this the world well knows: yet none knows well
To shun the heaven that leads men to this hell.

Sonnet 130

My mistress' eyes are nothing like the sun;
    Coral is far more red than her lips' red:
If snow be white, why then her breasts are dun;
    If hairs be wires, black wires grow on her head.
I have seen roses damasked, red and white,   5
    But no such roses see I in her cheeks;
And in some perfumes is there more delight
    Than in the breath that from my mistress reeks.
I love to hear her speak, yet well I know
    That music hath a far more pleasing sound;   10
I grant I never saw a goddess go –
    My mistress, when she walks, treads on the ground;
And yet, by heaven, I think my love as rare
As any she belied with false compare.

Sonnet 138

When my love swears that she is made of truth,
    I do believe her, though I know she lies;
That she might think me some untutored youth,
    Unlearned in the world's false subtleties
Thus vainly thinking that she thinks me young,   5
    Although she knows my days are past the best,
Simply I credit her false-speaking tongue;
    On both sides thus is simple truth suppressed.
But wherefore says she not she is unjust?
    And wherefore say not I that I am old?   10
Oh, love's best habit is in seeming trust,
    And age in love loves not to have years told.
Therefore I lie with her, and she with me,
And in our faults by lies we flattered be.

Sonnet 139

O call not me to justify the wrong
    That thy unkindness lays upon my heart;
Wound me not with thine eye but with thy tongue;
    Use power with power, and slay me not by art.
Tell me thou lov'st elsewhere; but in my sight,   5
    Dear heart, forbear to glance thine eye aside;
What need'st thou wound with cunning when thy might
    Is more than my o'erpressed defence can bide?
Let me excuse thee: "Ah, my love well knows
    Her pretty looks have been mine enemies,   10
And therefore from my face she turns my foes,

That they elsewhere might dart their injuries."
Yet do not so, but since I am near slain,
Kill me outright with looks, and rid my pain.

Sonnet 140

Be wise as thou art cruel, do not press
   My tongue-tied patience with too much disdain,
Lest sorrow lend me words, and words express
   The manner of my pity-wanting pain.
If I might teach thee wit, better it were,   5
   Though not to love, yet, love, to tell me so –
As testy sick men, when their deaths be near,
   No news but health from their physicians know.
For if I should despair I should grow mad,
   And in my madness might speak ill of thee;   10
Now this ill-wresting world is grown so bad,
   Mad slanderers by mad ears believèd be.
That I may not be so, nor thou belied,
Bear thine eyes straight, though thy proud heart go wide.

Sonnet 141

In faith, I do not love thee with mine eyes,
   For they in thee a thousand errors note,
But 'tis my heart that loves what they despise,
   Who in despite of view is pleased to dote.
Nor are mine ears with thy tongue's tune delighted,   5
   Nor tender feeling to base touches prone,
Nor taste, nor smell, desire to be invited
   To any sensual feast with thee alone;
But my five wits nor my five senses can
   Dissuade one foolish heart from serving thee,   10
Who leaves unswayed the likeness of a man,
   Thy proud heart's slave and vassal wretch to be.
Only my plague thus far I count my gain,
That she that makes me sin awards me pain.

Sonnet 147

My love is as a fever, longing still
   For that which longer nurseth the disease;
Feeding on that which doth preserve the ill,
   The uncertain sickly appetite to please.
My reason, the physician to my love,   5
   Angry that his prescriptions are not kept,
Hath left me, and I desperate now approve
   Desire is death, which physic did except.

Past cure I am, now reason is past care,
　And frantic mad with evermore unrest;   10
My thoughts and my discourse as mad men's are,
　At random from the truth vainly expressed;
For I have sworn thee fair, and thought thee bright,
Who art as black as hell, as dark as night.

Sonnet 148

Oh me! what eyes hath Love put in my head,
　Which have no correspondence with true sight –
Or, if they have, where is my judgment fled,
　That censures falsely what they see aright?
If that be fair whereon my false eyes dote,   5
　What means the world to say it is not so?
If it be not, then Love doth well denote
　Love's eye is not so true as all men's: no,
How can it? Oh how can Love's eye be true,
　That is so vexed with watching and with tears?   10
No marvel then though I mistake my view;
　The sun itself sees not, till heaven clears.
Oh cunning Love! with tears thou keep'st me blind,
Lest eyes well seeing thy foul faults should find.

Thomas Campion
(1567–1620)

Cherry-Ripe

There is a garden in her face
  Where roses and white lilies blow;
A heavenly paradise is that place,
  Wherein all pleasant fruits do flow:
    There cherries grow which none may buy   5
    Till 'Cherry-ripe' themselves do cry.

Those cherries fairly do enclose
  Of orient pearls a double row,
Which when her lovely laughter shows,
  They look like rose-buds filled with snow;   10
    Yet them nor peer nor prince can buy
    Till 'Cherry-ripe' themselves do cry.

Her eyes like angels watch them still;
  Her brows like bended bows do stand,
Threat'ning with piercing frowns to kill   15
  All that attempt with eye or hand
    Those sacred cherries to come nigh,
    Till 'Cherry-ripe' themselves do cry.

John Donne
(1572–1631)

Love's Deity

I long to talk with some old lover's ghost,
    Who died before the god of love was born:
I cannot think that he, who then loved most,
    Sunk so low as to love one which did scorn.
But since this god produced a destiny,   5
And that vice-nature, custom, lets it be,
    I must love her that loves not me.

Sure, they which made him god meant not so much,
    Nor he in his young godhead practised it;
But when an even flame two hearts did touch,   10
    His office was indulgently to fit
Actives to passives. Correspondency
Only his subject was; it cannot be
    Love, till I love her that loves me.

But every modern god will now extend   15
    His vast prerogative as far as Jove.
To rage, to lust, to write to, to commend,
    All is the purlieu of the god of love.
Oh, were we wakened by this tyranny
To ungod this child again, it could not be   20
    I should love her, who loves not me.

Rebel and atheist too, why murmur I,
    As though I felt the worst that love could do?
Love may make me leave loving, or might try
    A deeper plague, to make her love me too,   25
Which, since she loves before, I'm loath to see;
Falsehood is worse than hate; and that must be,
    If she whom I love, should love me.

Song

Go and catch a falling star,
    Get with child a mandrake root,

Tell me where all past years are,
   Or who cleft the devil's foot,
Teach me to hear mermaids singing,   5
   Or to keep off envy's stinging,
       And find
       What wind
Serves to advance an honest mind.

If thou beest born to strange sights,   10
   Things invisible to see,
Ride ten thousand days and nights,
   Till age snow white hairs on thee,
Thou, when thou return'st, wilt tell me
All strange wonders that befell thee,   15
       And swear
       No where
Lives a woman true, and fair.

If thou find'st one, let me know,
   Such a pilgrimage were sweet;   20
Yet do not, I would not go,
   Though at next door we might meet;
Though she were true when you met her,
And last till you write your letter,
       Yet she   25
       Will be
False, ere I come, to two or three.

Woman's Constancy

Now thou hast loved me one whole day,
Tomorrow when thou leav'st, what wilt thou say?
Wilt thou then antedate some new-made vow?
   Or say that now
We are not just those persons which we were?   5
Or, that oaths made in reverential fear
Of love, and his wrath, any may forswear?
Or, as true deaths true marriages untie,
So lovers' contracts, images of those,
Bind but till sleep, death's image, them unloose?   10
   Or, your own end to justify,
For having purposed change and falsehood, you
Can have no way but falsehood to be true?
Vain lunatic, against these scapes I could
   Dispute and conquer, if I would;   15
   Which I abstain to do,
For by tomorrow, I may think so too.

The Flea

Mark but this flea, and mark in this,
How little that which thou deny'st me is;
It sucked me first, and now sucks thee,
And in this flea our two bloods mingled be;
Thou know'st that this cannot be said   5
A sin, nor shame, nor loss of maidenhead;
   Yet this enjoys before it woo,
    And pampered swells with one blood made of two,
    And this, alas, is more than we would do.

Oh stay, three lives in one flea spare,   10
Where we almost, yea, more than married are.
This flea is you and I, and this
Our marriage bed, and marriage temple is;
Though parents grudge, and you, we are met,
And cloistered in these living walls of jet.   15
   Though use make you apt to kill me,
    Let not to that, self-murder added be,
    And sacrilege, three sins in killing three.

Cruel and sudden, hast thou since
Purpled thy nail in blood of innocence?   20
Wherein could this flea guilty be,
Except in that drop which it sucked from thee?
Yet thou triumph'st and say'st that thou
Find'st not thyself, nor me the weaker now;
   'Tis true, then learn how false fears be: 25
    Just so much honour, when thou yield'st to me,
    Will waste, as this flea's death took life from thee.

The Bait

Come live with me, and be my love,
And we will some new pleasures prove,
Of golden sands, and crystal brooks,
With silken lines, and silver hooks.

There will the river whispering run,   5
Warmed by thy eyes more than the sun.
And there the enamoured fish will stay,
Begging themselves they may betray.

When thou wilt swim in that live bath,
Each fish, which every channel hath,   10
Will amorously to thee swim,
Gladder to catch thee, than thou him.

If thou, to be so seen, beest loath,
By sun or moon, thou dark'nest both;
And if myself have leave to see,   15
I need not their light, having thee.

Let others freeze with angling reeds,
And cut their legs with shells and weeds,
Or treacherously poor fish beset
With strangling snare, or windowy net.   20

Let coarse bold hands from slimy nest
The bedded fish in banks out-wrest,
Or curious traitors, sleave-silk flies,
Bewitch poor fishes' wand'ring eyes.

For thee, thou need'st no such deceit,   25
For thou thyself art thine own bait;
That fish that is not catched thereby,
Alas, is wiser far than I.

The Will

Before I sigh my last gasp, let me breathe,
Great Love, some legacies: here I bequeath
Mine eyes to Argus, if mine eyes can see;
If they be blind, then Love, I give them thee;
My tongue to Fame; to ambassadors mine ears;   5
    To women or the sea, my tears.
    Thou, Love, hast taught me heretofore
By making me serve her who'had twenty more,
That I should give to none but such as had too much before.

My constancy I to the planets give;   10
My truth to them who at the court do live;
Mine ingenuity and openness
To Jesuits; to buffoons my pensiveness;
My silence to any who abroad hath been;
    My money to a Capuchin.   15
    Thou, Love, taught'st me, by appointing me
To love there where no love received can be,
Only to give to such as have an incapacity.

My faith I give to Roman Catholics;
All my good works unto the schismatics   20
Of Amsterdam; my best civility
And courtship to an University;
My modesty I give to soldiers bare;
    My patience let gamesters share.

Thou, Love, taught'st me, by making me   25
Love her that holds my love disparity,
Only to give to those that count my gifts indignity.

I give my reputation to those
Which were my friends; mine industry to foes;
To schoolmen I bequeath my doubtfulness;   30
My sickness to physicians, or excess;
To nature, all that I in rhyme have writ;
        And to my company my wit.
    Thou, Love, by making me adore
Her who begot this love in me before,   35
Taught'st me to make as though I gave, when I did but restore.

To him for whom the passing bell next tolls,
I give my physic books; my written rolls
Of moral counsels, I to Bedlam give;
My brazen medals unto them which live   40
In want of bread; to them which pass among
        All foreigners, mine English tongue.
    Thou, Love, by making me love one
Who thinks her friendship a fit portion
For younger lovers, dost my gifts thus disproportion.   45

Therefore I'll give no more, but I'll undo
The world by dying, because love dies too.
Then all your beauties will be no more worth
Than gold in mines, where none doth draw it forth;
And all your graces no more use shall have   50
        Than a sundial in a grave.
    Thou, Love, taught'st me, by making me
Love her who doth neglect both me and thee,
To invent, and practise this one way, to annihilate all three.

The Sun Rising

Busy old fool, unruly sun,
        Why dost thou thus
Through windows and through curtains call on us?
Must to thy motions lovers' seasons run?
        Saucy pedantic wretch, go chide   5
        Late schoolboys and sour prentices,
    Go tell court-huntsmen that the King will ride,
        Call country ants to harvest offices;
Love, all alike, no season knows, nor clime,
Nor hours, days, months, which are the rags of time.   10

Thy beams, so reverend and strong
  Why shouldst thou think?
I could eclipse and cloud them with a wink,
But that I would not lose her sight so long;
    If her eyes have not blinded thine,   15
    Look, and tomorrow late tell me
  Whether both the Indias of spice and mine
  Be where thou left'st them, or lie here with me.
Ask for those kings whom thou saw'st yesterday,
And thou shalt hear, all here in one bed lay.   20

    She is all states, and all princes I;
    Nothing else is.
Princes do but play us; compared to this,
All honour's mimic, all wealth alchemy.
    Thou, sun, art half as happy as we,   .   25
    In that the world's contracted thus;
  Thine age asks ease, and since thy duties be
  To warm the world, that's done in warming us.
Shine here to us, and thou art everywhere;
This bed thy centre is, these walls thy sphere.   30

The Computation

For the first twenty years, since yesterday,
I scarce believed thou couldst be gone away;
For forty more I fed on favours past,
And forty on hopes, that thou wouldst they might last.
Tears drowned one hundred, and sighs blew out two;   5
A thousand, I did neither think nor do,
Or not divide, all being one thought of you;
Or in a thousand more, forgot that too.
Yet call not this long life, but think that I
Am, by being dead, immortal; can ghosts die?   10

A Lecture upon the Shadow

Stand still, and I will read to thee
A lecture, love, in love's philosophy.
  These three hours that we have spent
  Walking here, two shadows went
Along with us, which we ourselves produced;   5
  But, now the sun is just above our head,
  We do those shadows tread,
And to brave clearness all things are reduced.
  So whilst our infant loves did grow,

Disguises did, and shadows, flow   10
From us and our cares, but now 'tis not so.

That love hath not attained the high'st degree,
Which is still diligent lest others see.
Except our loves at this noon stay,
We shall new shadows make the other way.   15
    As the first were made to blind
    Others, these which come behind
Will work upon ourselves, and blind our eyes.
    If our loves faint, and westwardly decline,
    To me thou falsely thine,   20
And I to thee, mine actions shall disguise.
    The morning shadows wear away,
    But these grow longer all the day;
    But oh, love's day is short, if love decay.

Love is a growing, or full constant light,   25
And his short minute after noon, is night.

Love's Alchemy

Some that have deeper digged love's mine than I,
Say where his centric happiness doth lie;
    I have loved, and got, and told,
But should I love, get, tell, till I were old,
I should not find that hidden mystery.   5
        Oh, 'tis imposture all,
And as no chemic yet the elixir got,
        But glorifies his pregnant pot
        If by the way to him befall
Some odoriferous thing, or medicinal,   10
    So lovers dream a rich and long delight,
    But get a winter-seeming summer's night.

Our ease, our thrift, our honour, and our day,
Shall we for this vain bubble's shadow pay?
        Ends love in this, that my man   15
Can be as happy as I can, if he can
Endure the short scorn of a bridegroom's play?
        That loving wretch that swears
'Tis not the bodies marry, but the minds,
        Which he in her angelic finds,
        Would swear as justly that he hears,   20
In that day's rude hoarse minstrelsy, the spheres.
    Hope not for mind in women: at their best,
    Sweetness and wit, they are but mummy possessed.

The Ecstasy

Where, like a pillow on a bed,
  A pregnant bank swelled up to rest
The violet's reclining head,
  Sat we two, one another's best.
Our hands were firmly cemented   5
  With a fast balm, which thence did spring;
Our eyebeams twisted, and did thread
  Our eyes upon one double string;
So to entergraft our hands, as yet
  Was all the means to make us one,   10
And pictures in our eyes to get
  Was all our propagation.
As 'twixt two equal armies fate
  Suspends uncertain victory,
Our souls, which to advance their state   15
  Were gone out, hung 'twixt her and me.
And whilst our souls negotiate there,
  We like sepulchral statues lay;
All day, the same our postures were,
  And we said nothing, all the day.   20
If any, so by love refined
  That he soul's language understood,
And by good love were grown all mind,
  Within convenient distance stood,
He, though he knew not which soul spake,   25
  Because both meant, both spake the same,
Might thence a new concoction take
  And part far purer than he came.
This ecstasy doth unperplex,
  We said, and tell us what we love: 30
We see by this it was not sex,
  We see we saw not what did move;
But as all several souls contain
  Mixture of things, they know not what,
Love these mixed souls doth mix again   35
  And makes both one, each this and that.
A single violet transplant,
  The strength, the colour, and the size,
All which before was poor and scant,
  Redoubles still, and multiplies.   40
When love with one another so
  Interinanimates two souls,
That abler soul, which thence doth flow,
  Defects of loneliness controls.
We then, who are this new soul, know   45

Of what we are composed and made,
For the atomies of which we grow
   Are souls, whom no change can invade.
But oh, alas, so long, so far,
   Our bodies why do we forbear?   50
They are ours, though not we; we are
   The intelligences, they the sphere.
We owe them thanks, because they thus
   Did us to us at first convey,
Yielded their forces, sense, to us,   55
   Nor are dross to us, but allay.
On man heaven's influence works not so,
   But that it first imprints the air;
For soul into the soul may flow,
   Though it to body first repair.   60
As our blood labours to beget
   Spirits, as like souls as it can,
Because such fingers need to knit
   That subtle knot which makes us man,
So must pure lovers' souls descend   65
   To affections, and to faculties,
Which sense may reach and apprehend,
   Else a great prince in prison lies.
To our bodies turn we then, that so
   Weak men on love revealed may look;   70
Love's mysteries in souls do grow,
   But yet the body is his book.
And if some lover, such as we,
   Have heard this dialogue of one,
Let him still mark us, he shall see   75
   Small change when we are to bodies gone.

The Good-Morrow

I wonder by my troth, what thou and I
Did, till we loved? Were we not weaned till then,
But sucked on country pleasures, childishly?
Or snorted we in the seven sleepers' den?
'Twas so; but this, all pleasures fancies be.   5
If ever any beauty I did see,
Which I desired, and got, 'twas but a dream of thee.

And now good morrow to our waking souls,
Which watch not one another out of fear;
For love all love of other sights controls,   10
And makes one little room an everywhere.
Let sea-discoverers to new worlds have gone,

Let maps to other, worlds on worlds have shown;
Let us possess one world, each hath one, and is one.

My face in thine eye, thine in mine appears,   15
And true plain hearts do in the faces rest;
Where can we find two better hemispheres
Without sharp north, without declining west?
Whatever dies was not mixed equally;
If our two loves be one, or thou and I   20
Love so alike that none do slacken, none can die.

Air and Angels

Twice or thrice had I loved thee,
Before I knew thy face or name;
So in a voice, so in a shapeless flame,
Angels affect us oft, and worshipped be;
   Still when, to where thou wert, I came,   5
Some lovely glorious nothing I did see.
   But since my soul, whose child love is,
Takes limbs of flesh, and else could nothing do,
    More subtle than the parent is
Love must not be, but take a body too;   10
    And therefore what thou wert, and who,
      I bid love ask, and now
That it assume thy body I allow,
And fix itself in thy lip, eye, and brow.

Whilst thus to ballast love I thought,   15
And so more steadily to have gone,
With wares which would sink admiration,
I saw I had love's pinnace overfraught;
   Every thy hair for love to work upon
Is much too much, some fitter must be sought;   20
   For, nor in nothing, nor in things
Extreme and scattering bright, can love inhere;
   Then as an angel, face and wings
Of air, not pure as it, yet pure doth wear,
    So thy love may be my love's sphere;   25
      Just such disparity
As is 'twixt air and angels' purity,
'Twixt women's love and men's will ever be.

The Prohibition

    Take heed of loving me;
At least remember, I forbade it thee;

Not that I shall repair my unthrifty waste
Of breath and blood, upon thy sighs and tears,
By being to thee then what to me thou wast;   5
But so great joy our life at once outwears;
Then, lest thy love by my death frustrate be,
If thou love me, take heed of loving me.

    Take heed of hating me,
Or too much triumph in the victory.   10
Not that I shall be mine own officer,
And hate with hate again retaliate;
But thou wilt lose the style of conqueror,
If I, thy conquest, perish by thy hate.
Then, lest my being nothing lessen thee,   15
If thou hate me, take heed of hating me.

    Yet love and hate me too,
So these extremes shall ne'er their office do:
Love me, that I may die the gentler way,
Hate me, because thy love is too great for me,   20
Or let these two, themselves not me decay;
So shall I live, thy stage not triumph be;
Lest thou thy love and hate and me undo,
To let me live, oh love and hate me too.

Lovers' Infiniteness

If yet I have not all thy love,
Dear, I shall never have it all;
I cannot breathe one other sigh to move,
Nor can entreat one other tear to fall,
And all my treasure, which should purchase thee,   5
Sighs, tears, and oaths, and letters, I have spent.
Yet no more can be due to me
Than at the bargain made was meant;
If then thy gift of love were partial,
That some to me, some should to others fall,   10
    Dear, I shall never have thee all.

Or if then thou gavest me all,
All was but all, which thou hadst then;
But if in thy heart since there be, or shall
New love created be, by other men   15
Which have their stocks entire, and can in tears,
In sighs, in oaths, and letters outbid me,
This new love may beget new fears,
For this love was not vowed by thee.

And yet it was, thy gift being general;   20
The ground, thy heart, is mine; whatever shall
   Grow there, dear, I should have it all.

Yet I would not have all yet;
He that hath all can have no more,
And since my love doth every day admit   25
New growth, thou shouldst have new rewards in store;
Thou canst not every day give me thy heart,
If thou canst give it, then thou never gavest it;
Love's riddles are, that though thy heart depart,
It stays at home, and thou with losing savest it;   30
But we will have a way more liberal
Than changing hearts to join them, so we shall
   Be one, and one another's all.

Love's Growth

I scarce believe my love to be so pure
      As I had thought it was,
      Because it doth endure
Vicissitude, and season, as the grass;
Methinks I lied all winter, when I swore   5
My love was infinite, if spring make it more.
But if this medicine, love, which cures all sorrow
With more, not only be no quintessence,
But mixed of all stuffs, paining soul or sense,
And of the sun his working vigour borrow,   10
Love's not so pure and abstract as they use
To say, which have no mistress but their muse;
But as all else, being elemented too,
Love sometimes would contemplate, sometimes do.

And yet no greater, but more eminent,   15
      Love by the spring is grown;
      As in the firmament,
Stars by the sun are not enlarged, but shown.
Gentle love-deeds, as blossoms on a bough,
From love's awakened root do bud out now.   20
If, as in water stirred more circles be
Produced by one, love such additions take,
Those like so many spheres but one heaven make,
For they are all concentric unto thee.
And though each spring do add to love new heat,   25
As princes do in times of action get
New taxes, and remit them not in peace,
No winter shall abate the spring's increase.

The Anniversary

All kings, and all their favourites,
  All glory of honours, beauties, wits,
The sun itself, which makes times as they pass,
Is elder by a year now, than it was
When thou and I first one another saw;   5
All other things to their destruction draw,
    Only our love hath no decay;
This no tomorrow hath, nor yesterday,
Running, it never runs from us away,
But truly keeps his first, last, everlasting day.   10

    Two graves must hide thine and my corse;
    If one might, death were no divorce.
Alas, as well as other princes, we,
Who prince enough in one another be,
Must leave at last in death these eyes and ears,   15
Oft fed with true oaths, and with sweet salt tears;
    But souls where nothing dwells but love,
All other thoughts being inmates, then shall prove
This, or a love increased there above,
When bodies to their graves, souls from their graves, remove.   20

    And then we shall be throughly blest,
    But we no more than all the rest;
Here upon earth we're kings, and none but we
Can be such kings, nor of such subjects be.
Who is so safe as we, where none can do   25
Treason to us, except one of us two?
    True and false fears let us refrain;
Let us love nobly, and live, and add again
Years and years unto years, till we attain
To write threescore; this is the second of our reign.   30

The Canonization

For God's sake hold your tongue, and let me love,
  Or chide my palsy, or my gout,
My five gray hairs, or ruined fortune flout;
    With wealth your state, your mind with arts improve,
    Take you a course, get you a place,   5
    Observe his honour, or his grace;
Or the king's real, or his stamped face
  Contemplate; what you will, approve,
  So you will let me love.

Alas, alas, who's injured by my love?   10
   What merchants' ships have my sighs drowned?
Who says my tears have overflowed his ground?
   When did my colds a forward spring remove?
      When did the heats which my veins fill
      Add one more to the plaguy bill?   15
Soldiers find wars, and lawyers find out still
   Litigious men, which quarrels move,
   Though she and I do love.

Call us what you will, we are made such by love;
   Call her one, me another fly,   20
We are tapers too, and at our own cost die,
   And we in us find the eagle and the dove.
      The phoenix riddle hath more wit
      By us; we two being one, are it.
So to one neutral thing both sexes fit,   25
   We die and rise the same, and prove
   Mysterious by this love.

We can die by it, if not live by love,
   And if unfit for tombs and hearse
Our legend be, it will be fit for verse;   30
   And if no piece of chronicle we prove,
      We'll build in sonnets pretty rooms;
      As well a well-wrought run becomes
The greatest ashes, as half-acre tombs,
   And by these hymns, all shall approve   35
   Us canonized for love,

And thus invoke us: You whom reverend love
   Made one another's hermitage;
You, to whom love was peace, that now is rage;
   Who did the whole world's soul contract, and drove   40
      Into the glasses of your eyes –
      So made such mirrors and such spies
That they did all to you epitomize,–
   Countries, towns, courts; beg from above
   A pattern of your love!   45

A Valediction: Of Weeping

   Let me pour forth
My tears before thy face whilst I stay here,
For thy face coins them, and thy stamp they bear,
And by this mintage they are something worth,
   For thus they be   5

    Pregnant of thee;
Fruits of much grief they are, emblems of more –
When a tear falls, that thou fallst which it bore,
So thou and I are nothing then, when on a diverse shore.

    On a round ball   10
A workman that hath copies by, can lay
An Europe, Afric, and an Asia,
And quickly make that which was nothing, all;
    So doth each tear
    Which thee doth wear,   15
A globe, yea world, by that impression grow,
Till thy tears mixed with mine do overflow
This world; by waters sent from thee, my heaven dissolved so.

    O more than moon,
Draw not up seas to drown me in thy sphere;   20
Weep me not dead, in thine arms, but forbear
To teach the sea what it may do too soon;
    Let not the wind
    Example find,
To do me more harm than it purposeth;   25
Since thou and I sigh one another's breath,
Whoe'er sighs most is cruellest, and hastes the other's death.

A Valediction: Forbidding Mourning

As virtuous men pass mildly away,
    And whisper to their souls to go,
Whilst some of their sad friends do say,
    The breath goes now, and some say, No;

So let us melt, and make no noise,   5
    No tear-floods, nor sigh-tempests move;
'Twere profanation of our joys
    To tell the laity our love.

Moving of the earth brings harms and fears,
    Men reckon what it did and meant;   10
But trepidation of the spheres,
    Though greater far, is innocent.

Dull sublunary lovers' love,
    Whose soul is sense, cannot admit
Absence, because it doth remove   15
    Those things which elemented it.

But we by a love so much refined
  That ourselves know not what it is,
Inter-assured of the mind,
  Care less eyes, lips, hands to miss.   20

Our two souls therefore, which are one,
  Though I must go, endure not yet
A breach, but an expansion,
  Like gold to airy thinness beat.

If they be two, they are two so   25
  As stiff twin compasses are two;
Thy soul, the fixed foot, makes no show
  To move, but doth if the other do.

And though it in the centre sit,
  Yet when the other far doth roam,   30
It leans, and hearkens after it,
  And grows erect as that comes home.

Such wilt thou be to me who must,
  Like the other foot, obliquely run;
Thy firmness makes my circle just,   35
  And makes me end where I begun.

The Funeral

Whoever comes to shroud me, do not harm
  Nor question much
That subtle wreath of hair which crowns my arm;
The mystery, the sign you must not touch,
  For 'tis my outward soul,   5
Viceroy to that, which unto heaven being gone,
  Will leave this to control
And keep these limbs, her provinces, from dissolution.

For if the sinewy thread my brain lets fall
  Through every part,   10
Can tie those parts, and make me one of all,
Those hairs, which upward grew, and strength and art
  Have from a better brain,
Can better do it; except she meant that I
  By this should know my pain,   15
As prisoners then are manacled, when they are condemned to die.

Whate'er she meant by it, bury it with me,
  For since I am

Love's martyr, it might breed idolatry
If into others' hands these relics came;   20
    As 'twas humility
To afford to it all that a soul can do,
    So 'tis some bravery,
That since you would have none of me, I bury some of you.

The Relic

When my grave is broke up again
Some second guest to entertain—
For graves have learned that womanhead,
To be to more than one a bed—
    And he that digs it, spies   5
A bracelet of bright hair about the bone,
    Will he not let us alone,
And think that there a loving couple lies,
Who thought that this device might be some way
To make their souls, at the last busy day,   10
Meet at this grave, and make a little stay?

If this fall in a time or land
Where mis-devotion doth command,
Then he that digs us up will bring
Us to the bishop and the king,   15
    To make us relics; then
Thou shalt be a Mary Magdalen, and I
    A something else thereby;
All women shall adore us, and some men;
And since at such time miracles are sought,   20
I would have that age by this paper taught
What miracles we harmless lovers wrought.

First, we loved well and faithfully,
Yet knew not what we loved, nor why,
Difference of sex no more we knew   25
    Than our guardian angels do;
    Coming and going, we
Perchance might kiss, but not between those meals;
    Our hands ne'er touched the seals,
Which nature, injured by late law, sets free;   30
These miracles we did, but now alas,
All measure and all language I should pass,
Should I tell what a miracle she was.

Twicknam Garden

Blasted with sighs, and surrounded with tears,
    Hither I come to seek the spring,
    And at mine eyes, and at mine ears,
Receive such balms as else cure everything;
    But oh, self traitor, I do bring   5
The spider love, which transubstantiates all,
    And can convert manna to gall;
And that this place may thoroughly be thought
    True paradise, I have the serpent brought.

'Twere wholesomer for me that winter did   10
    Benight the glory of this place,
    And that a grave frost did forbid
These trees to laugh and mock me to my face;
    But that I may not this disgrace
Endure, nor yet leave loving, Love, let me   15
    Some senseless piece of this place be;
Make me a mandrake, so I may groan here,
    Or a stone fountain weeping out my year.

Hither with crystal vials, lovers, come
    And take my tears, which are love's wine,   20
    And try your mistress' tears at home,
For all are false that taste not just like mine;
    Alas, hearts do not in eyes shine,
Nor can you more judge woman's thoughts by tears,
    Than by her shadow what she wears.   25
O perverse sex, where none is true but she,
    Who's therefore true, because her truth kills me.

A Nocturnal upon St Lucy's Day,
being the Shortest Day

'Tis the year's midnight, and it is the day's,
Lucy's, who scarce seven hours herself unmasks;
   The sun is spent, and now his flasks
   Send forth light squibs, no constant rays;
    The world's whole sap is sunk;   5
The general balm the hydroptic earth hath drunk,
Whither, as to the bed's feet, life is shrunk,
Dead and interred; yet all these seem to laugh,
Compared with me, who am their epitaph.

Study me then, you who shall lovers be   10
At the next world, that is, at the next spring;

For I am every dead thing,
  In whom Love wrought new alchemy.
    For his art did express
A quintessence even from nothingness,   15
From dull privations, and lean emptiness;
He ruined me, and I am re-begot
Of absence, darkness, death—things which are not.

All others from all things draw all that's good,
Life, soul, form, spirit, whence they being have;   20
  I, by Love's limbec, am the grave
  Of all that's nothing. Oft a flood
    Have we two wept, and so
Drowned the whole world, us two; oft did we grow
To be two chaoses, when we did show   25
Care to aught else; and often absences
Withdrew our souls, and made us carcasses.

But I am by her death, which word wrongs her,
Of the first nothing the elixir grown;
  Were I a man, that I were one   30
  I needs must know; I should prefer,
    If I were any beast,
Some ends, some means; yea plants, yea stones detest
And love; all, all some properties invest;
If I an ordinary nothing were,   35
As shadow, a light and body must be here.

But I am none; nor will my sun renew.
You lovers, for whose sake the lesser sun
  At this time to the Goat is run
  To fetch new lust, and give it you,   40
    Enjoy your summer all;
Since she enjoys her long night's festival,
Let me prepare towards her, and let me call
This hour her vigil, and her eve, since this
Both the year's and the day's deep midnight is.   45

To his Mistress Going to Bed

Come, Madam, come, all rest my powers defy,
Until I labour, I in labour lie.
The foe oft-times having the foe in sight,
Is tired with standing though they never fight.
Off with that girdle, like heaven's zone glistering,   5
But a far fairer world encompassing.
Unpin that spangled breastplate which you wear,
That the eyes of busy fools may be stopped there.

Unlace yourself, for that harmonious chime
Tells me from you, that now 'tis your bedtime.   10
Off with that happy busk, which I envy,
That still can be, and still can stand so nigh.
Your gown going off, such beauteous state reveals,
As when from flowery meads the hill's shadow steals.
Off with that wiry coronet and show   15
The hairy diadem which on you doth grow;
Now off with those shoes, and then safely tread
In this love's hallowed temple, this soft bed.
In such white robes heaven's angels used to be
Received by men; thou angel bring'st with thee   20
A heaven like Mahomet's paradise; and though
Ill spirits walk in white, we easily know
By this these angels from an evil sprite:
Those set our hairs, but these our flesh upright.
　　Licence my roving hands, and let them go   25
Before, behind, between, above, below.
O my America, my newfound land,
My kingdom, safeliest when with one man manned,
My mine of precious stones, my empery,
How blessed am I in this discovering thee!   30
To enter in these bonds, is to be free;
Then where my hand is set, my seal shall be.
　　Full nakedness, all joys are due to thee.
As souls unbodied, bodies unclothed must be,
To taste whole joys. Gems which you women use   35
Are like Atlanta's balls, cast in men's views,
That when a fool's eye lighteth on a gem,
His earthly soul may covet theirs, not them.
Like pictures, or like books' gay coverings made
For laymen, are all women thus arrayed;   40
Themselves are mystic books, which only we
Whom their imputed grace will dignify
Must see revealed. Then since I may know,
As liberally, as to a midwife, show
Thyself: cast all, yea, this white linen hence,   45
Here is no penance, much less innocence.
　　To teach thee, I am naked first, why then
What needst thou have more covering than a man.

From *Holy Sonnets*

Sonnet 6

Death be not proud, though some have called thee
　　Mighty and dreadful, for thou art not so,

For those whom thou think'st thou dost overthrow,
Die not, poor death, nor yet canst thou kill me.
From rest and sleep, which but thy pictures be,   5
Much pleasure, then from thee, much more must flow,
And soonest our best men with thee do go,
Rest of their bones, and souls deliverie.
Thou art slave to Fate, Chance, kings, and desperate men,
And dost with poison, war, and sickness dwell,   10
And poppy, or charms can make us sleep as well,
And better then thy stroke; why swell'st thou then?
One short sleep past, we wake eternally,
And death shall be no more; death, thou shalt die.

Sonnet 10

Batter my heart, three-personed God, for you
As yet but knock, breathe, shine, and seek to mend;
That I may rise and stand, o'erthrow me; and bend
Your force to break, blow, burn, and make me new.
I, like an usurped tower to another due,   5
Labour to admit you, but oh, to no end.
Reason, your viceroy in me, me should defend,
But is captived, and proves weak or untrue.
Yet dearly I love you, and would be loved fain,
But am betrothed unto your enemy;   10
Divorce me, untie or break that knot again;
Take me to you, imprison me, for I,
Except you enthrall me, never shall be free,
Nor ever chaste, except you ravish me.

Good Friday, 1613. Riding westward

Let man's soul be a sphere, and then in this
The intelligence that moves, devotion is;
And as the other spheres, by being grown
Subject to foreign motion, lose their own,
And being by others hurried every day   5
Scarce in a year their natural form obey,
Pleasure or business, so, our souls admit
For their first mover, and are whirled by it.
Hence is 't that I am carried towards the west
This day, when my soul's form bends towards the east.   10
There I should see a sun, by rising set,
And by that setting, endless day beget;
But that Christ on this cross did rise and fall,
Sin had eternally benighted all.
Yet dare I almost be glad I do not see   15

That spectacle of too much weight for me.
Who sees God's face, that is self life, must die;
What a death were it then to see God die!
It made his own lieutenant, nature, shrink;
It made his footstool crack, and the sun wink.   20
Could I behold those hands which span the poles
And tune all spheres at once, pierced with those holes?
Could I behold that endless height, which is
Zenith to us and our antipodes,
Humbled below us? or that blood which is   25
The seat of all our souls, if not of his,
Made dirt of dust, or that flesh which was worn
By God for his apparel, ragged and torn?
If on these things I durst not look, durst I
Upon his miserable mother cast mine eye,   30
Who was God's partner here, and furnished thus
Half of that sacrifice which ransomed us?
Though these things, as I ride, be from mine eye,
They're present yet unto my memory,
For that looks towards them; and thou look'st towards me,   35
O Saviour, as thou hang'st upon the tree;
I turn my back to thee but to receive
Corrections, till thy mercies bid thee leave.
Oh, think me worth thine anger, punish me,
Burn off my rusts, and my deformity;   40
Restore thine image, so much, by thy grace,
That thou mayst know me, and I'll turn my face.

A Hymn to God the Father

Wilt thou forgive that sin where I begun,
   Which was my sin, though it were done before?
Wilt thou forgive that sin through which I run,
   And do run still, though still I do deplore?
      When thou hast done, thou has not done,   5
         For I have more.

Wilt thou forgive that sin which I have won
   Others to sin, and made my sin their door?
Wilt thou forgive that sin which I did shun
   A year or two, but wallowed in a score?   10
      When thou hast done, thou hast not done,
         For I have more.

I have a sin of fear, that when I have spun
   My last thread, I shall perish on the shore;
But swear by thyself, that at my death thy Son   15

Shall shine as he shines now, and heretofore;
And having done that, thou hast done;
I fear no more.

Hymn to God, my God, in my Sickness

Since I am coming to that holy room
  Where, with thy choir of saints for evermore,
I shall be made thy music, as I come
  I tune the instrument here at the door,
  And what I must do then, think here before.   5

Whilst my physicians by their love are grown
  Cosmographers, and I their map, who lie
Flat on this bed, that by them may be shown
  That this is my south-west discovery,
  Per fretum febris, by these straits to die,   10

I joy, that in these straits I see my west;
  For though their currents yield return to none,
What shall my west hurt me? As west and east
  In all flat maps, and I am one, are one,
  So death doth touch the resurrection.   15

Is the Pacific sea my home? or are
  The eastern riches? is Jerusalem?
Anyan and Magellan and Gibraltar,
  All straits, and none but straits, are ways to them,
  Whether where Japhet dwelt, or Cham, or Shem.   20

We think that Paradise and Calvary,
  Christ's cross and Adam's tree, stood in one place;
Look, Lord, and find both Adams met in me:
  As the first Adam's sweat surrounds my face,
  May the last Adam's blood my soul embrace.   25

So, in his purple wrapped, receive me, Lord;
  By these, his thorns, give me his other crown;
And as to others' souls I preached thy word,
  Be this my text, my sermon to mine own:
  Therefore that he may raise, the Lord throws down.   30

Ben Jonson
(?1573–1637)

From *Epigrams*

On Court-Worm

All men are worms; but this no man. In silk
'Twas brought to court first wrapt, and white as milk;
Where, afterwards, it grew a butterfly,
Which was a caterpillar; so 'twill die.

On my First Daughter

Here lies, to each her parents ruth,
MARY, the daughter of their youth;
Yet all heaven's gifts being heaven's due,
It makes the father less to rue.
At six months end she parted hence   5
With safety of her innocence;
Whose soul heaven's Queen, whose name she bears,
In comfort of her mother's tears,
Hath placed amongst her virgin-train:
Where while that severed doth remain,   10
This grave partakes the fleshly birth;
Which cover lightly, gentle earth!

On my First Son

Farewell, thou child of my right hand, and joy;
My sin was too much hope of thee, loved boy:
Seven years thou wert lent to me, and I thee pay,
Exacted by thy fate, on the just day.
O, could I lose all father, now! for why   5
Will man lament the state he should envy?
To have so soon scaped world's, and flesh's rage,
And if no other misery, yet age!
Rest in soft peace, and asked, say here doth lie
BEN JONSON his best piece of Poetry: 10

For whose sake-henceforth all his vows be such,
As what he loves may never like too much.

On Gut

Gut eats all day and lechers all the night,
   So all his meat he tasteth over twice;
And striving so to double his delight,
   He makes himself a thorough-fare of vice.
Thus, in his belly, can he change a sin,   5
Lust it comes out, that gluttony went in.

From *The Forest*

To Penshurst

Thou art not, Penshurst, built to envious show
   Of touch or marble, nor canst boast a row
Of polished pillars, or a roof of gold;
   Thou hast no lantern whereof tales are told,
Or stairs or courts; but stand'st an ancient pile,   5
   And these, grudged at, art reverenced the while.
Thou joy'st in better marks, of soil, of air,
   Of wood, of water; therein thou art fair.
Thou hast thy walks for health as well as sport;
   Thy mount, to which the Dryads do resort,   10
Where Pan and Bacchus their high feasts have made
   Beneath the broad beech, and the chestnut shade,
That taller tree, which of a nut was set
   At his great birth, where all the Muses met.
There in the writhed bark are cut the names   15
   Of many a sylvan, taken with his flames;
And thence the ruddy satyrs oft provoke
   The lighter fauns to reach thy Lady's oak.
Thy copse too, named of Gamage, thou hast there,
   That never fails to serve thee seasoned deer   20
When thou wouldst feast, or exercise thy friends.
   The lower land, that to the river bends,
Thy sheep, thy bullocks, kine, and calves do feed;
   The middle grounds thy mares and horses breed.
Each bank doth yield thee conies; and the tops,   25
   Fertile of wood, Ashore and Sidney's copse,
To crown thy open table, doth provide
   The purpled pheasant with the speckled side;
The painted partridge lies in every field,
   And, for thy mess, is willing to be killed.   30

And if the high-swollen Medway fail thy dish,
    Thou hast thy ponds that pay thee tribute fish,
Fat aged carps that run into thy net,
    And pikes, now weary their own kind to eat,
As loath the second draught or cast to stay,   35
    Officiously at first themselves betray;
Bright eels that emulate them, and leap on land
    Before the fisher, or into his hand.
Then hath thy orchard fruit, thy garden flowers
    Fresh as the air, and new as are the hours.   40
The early cherry, with the later plum,
    Fig, grape, and quince, each in his time doth come;
The blushing apricot and woolly peach
    Hang on thy walls, that every child may reach.
And though thy walls be of the country stone,   45
    They are reared with no man's ruin, no man's groan;
There's none that dwell about them wish them down,
    But all come in, the farmer and the clown,
And no one empty handed, to salute
    Thy lord and lady, though they have no suit.   50
Some bring a capon, some a rural cake,
    Some nuts, some apples; some that think they make
The better cheeses bring 'em, or else send
    By their ripe daughters whom they would commend
This way to husbands, and whose baskets bear   55
    An emblem of themselves in plum or pear.
But what can this, more than express their love,
    Add to thy free provisions, far above
The need of such, whose liberal board doth flow
    With all that hospitality doth know?   60
Where comes no guest but is allowed to eat
    Without his fear, and of thy lord's own meat;
Where the same beer and bread, and self-same wine
    That is his lordship's shall be also mine.
And I not fain to sit, as some this day   65
    At great men's tables, and yet dine away.
Here no man tells my cups, nor, standing by,
    A waiter doth my gluttony envy,
But gives me what I call and lets me eat;
    He knows below he shall find plenty of meat.   70
Thy tables hoard not up for the next day,
    Nor when I take my lodging need I pray
For fire or lights or livery; all is there
    As if thou then wert mine, or I reigned here;
There's nothing I can wish, for which I stay.   75
    That found King James, when hunting late this way
With his brave son, the prince, they saw thy fires
    Shine bright on every hearth as the desires

Of thy Penates had been set on flame
    To entertain them, or the country came   80
With all their zeal to warm their welcome here.
    What great I will not say, but sudden cheer
Didst thou then make 'em! and what praise was heaped
    On thy good lady then! who therein reaped
The just reward of her high huswifery;   85
    To have her linen, plate, and all things nigh
When she was far, and not a room but dressed
    As if it had expected such a guest!
These, Penshurst, are thy praise, and yet not all.
    Thy lady's noble, fruitful, chaste withal;   90
His children thy great lord may call his own,
    A fortune in this age but rarely known.
They are and have been taught religion; thence
    Their gentler spirits have sucked innocence.
Each morn and even they are taught to pray   95
    With the whole household, and may every day
Read, in their virtuous parents' noble parts,
    The mysteries of manners, arms, and arts.
Now, Penshurst, they that will proportion thee
    With other edifices when they see   100
Those proud, ambitious heaps and nothing else,
    May say, their lords have built, but thy lord dwells.

To Sir Robert Wroth

How blest art thou, canst love the country, WROTH,
    Whether by choice, or fate, or both!
And though so near the city, and the court,
    Art ta'en with neither's vice nor sport:
That at great times, art no ambitious guest   5
    Of sheriff's dinner, or mayor's feast.
Nor com'st to view the better cloth of state,
    The richer hangings, or crown-plate;
Nor throng'st (when masquing is) to have a sight
    Of the short bravery of the night;   10
To view the jewels, stuffs, the pains, the wit
    There wasted, some not paid for yet!
But canst at home, in thy securer rest,
    Live, with unbought provision blest;
Free from proud porches, or the gilded roofs,   15
    'Mongst lowing herds and solid hoofs:
Along the curled woods, and painted meads,
    Through which a serpent river leads
To some cool courteous shade which he calls his,
    And makes sleep softer than it is.   20

Or if thou list the night in watch to break,
    A-bed canst hear the loud stag speak,
In spring, oft roused for thy master's sport,
    Who for it makes thy house his court;
Or with thy friends, the heart of all the year   25
    Divid'st, upon the lesser deer:
In autumn, at the partridge mak'st a flight,
    And giv'st thy gladder guests the sight;
And in the winter, hunt'st the flying hare,
    More for thy exercise than fare;   30
While all that follow, their glad ears apply
    To the full greatness of the cry:
Or hawking at the river, or the bush,
    Or shooting at the greedy thrush,
Thou dost with some delight the day outwear,   35
    Although the coldest of the year!
The whilst the several seasons thou hast seen
    Of flowery fields, of cop'ces green,
The mowed meadows, with the fleeced sheep,
    And feasts, that either shearers keep;   40
The ripened ears, yet humble in their height,
    And furrows laden with their weight;
The apple-harvest, that doth longer last;
    The hogs returned home fat from mast;
The trees cut out in log, and those boughs made   45
    A fire now, that lent a shade!
Thus Pan and Sylvan having had their rites,
    Comus puts in for new delights;
And fills thy open hall with mirth and cheer,
    As if in Saturn's reign it were;   50
Apollo's harp and Hermes' lyre resound,
    Nor are the Muses strangers found.
The rout of rural folk come thronging in,
    (Their rudeness then is thought no sin)
Thy noblest spouse affords them welcome grace;   55
    And the great heroes of her race
Sit mixt with loss of state, or reverence.
    Freedom doth with degree dispense.
The jolly wassal walks the often round,
    And in their cups their cares are drowned: 60
They think not then, which side the cause shall leese,
    Nor how to get the lawyer fees.
Such and no other was that age of old,
    Which boasts t' have had the head of gold.
And such, since thou canst make thine own content,   65
    Strive, Wroth, to live long innocent.
Let others watch in guilty arms, and stand
    The fury of a rash command,

Go enter breaches, meet the cannon's rage,
    That they may sleep with scars in age;   70
And shew their feathers shot, and colours torn,
    And brag that they were therefore born.
Let this man sweat, and wrangle at the bar,
    For every price, in every jar,
And change possessions oftener with his breath,   75
    Than either money, war, or death:
Let him than hardest sires more disinherit,
    And each where boast it as his merit
To blow up orphans, widows, and their states;
    And think his power doth equal Fate's.   80
Let that go heap a mass of wretched wealth,
    Purchased by rapine, worse than stealth,
And brooding o'er it sit with broadest eyes,
    Not doing good scarce when he dies.
Let thousands more go flatter vice, and win,   85
    By being organs to great sin;
Get place and honour, and be glad to keep
    The secrets that shall break their sleep:
And so they ride in purple, eat in plate,
    Though poison, think it a great fate.   90
But thou, my Wroth, if I can truth apply,
    Shalt neither that nor this envy:
Thy peace is made; and when man's state is well,
    'Tis better if he there can dwell.
God wisheth none should wreck on a strange shelf: 95
    To him man's dearer than t' himself,
And howsoever we may think things sweet,
    He always gives what he knows meet;
Which who can use is happy: such be thou.
    Thy morning's and thy evening's vow   100
Be thanks to Him, and earnest prayer, to find
    A body sound, with sounder mind;
To do thy country service, thyself right;
    That neither want do thee affright,
Nor death; but when thy latest sand is spent,   105
    Thou mayst think life a thing but lent.

Song

To Celia

Drink to me only with thine eyes,
    And I will pledge with mine;
Or leave a kiss but in the cup,
    And I'll not look for wine.

The thirst that from the soul doth rise,   5
   Doth ask a drink divine:
But might I of Jove's nectar sup,
   I would not change for thine.
I sent thee late a rosy wreath,
   Not so much honouring thee,   10
As giving it a hope, that there
   It could not withered be.
But thou thereon didst only breathe,
   And sent'st it back to me:
Since when it grows, and smells, I swear,   15
   Not of itself, but thee.

Epistle

To Katharine, Lady Aubigny

'Tis grown almost a danger to speak true
Of any good mind now; there are so few.
The bad, by number are so fortified,
As what they have lost t' expect, they dare deride.
So both the praised and praisers suffer; yet,   5
For others ill ought none their good forget.
I therefore, who profess myself in love
With every virtue, wheresoe'er it move,
And howsoever; as I am at feud
With sin and vice, though with a throne endued;   10
And, in this name, am given out dangerous
By arts and practice of the vicious,
Such as suspect themselves, and think it fit,
For their own capital crimes, to indict my wit;
I that have suffered this; and though forsook   15
Of Fortune, have not altered yet my look,
Or so my self abandoned, as because
Men are not just, or keep no holy laws
Of nature and society, I should faint;
Or fear to draw true lines, 'cause others paint: 20
I, madam, am become your praiser; where,
If it may stand with your soft blush to hear
Your self but told unto your self, and see
In my character what your features be,
You will not from the paper slightly pass: 25
No lady but at some time loves her glass.
And this shall be no false one, but as much
Removed as you from need to have it such.
Look then, and see your self—I will not say
Your beauty, for you see that every day;   30

And so do many more: all which can call
It perfect, proper, pure and natural,
Not taken up o' the doctors, but as well
As I, can say and see it doth excel;
That asks but to be censured by the eyes: 35
And in those outward forms all fools are wise.
Nor that your beauty wanted not a dower,
Do I reflect. Some alderman has power,
Or cozening farmer of the customs, so
To advance his doubtful issue, and o'erflow   40
A prince's fortune: these are gifts of chance,
And raise not virtue; they may vice enhance.
My mirror is more subtle, clear, refined,
And takes and gives the beauties of the mind;
Though it reject not those of Fortune: such   45
As blood, and match. Wherein, how more than much
Are you engaged to your happy fate,
For such a lot! that mixt you with a state
Of so great title, birth, but virtue most,
Without which all the rest were sounds, or lost.   50
'Tis only that can time and chance defeat:
For he that once is good, is ever great.
Wherewith then, madam, can you better pay
This blessing of your stars, than by that way
Of virtue which you tread? What if alone,   55
Without companions? 'tis safe to have none.
In single paths dangers with ease are watched;
Contagion in the press is soonest catched.
This makes, that wisely you decline your life
Far from the maze of custom, error, strife,   60
And keep an even, and unaltered gait;
Not looking by or back, like those that wait
Times and occasions, to start forth, and seem,
Which, though the turning world may disesteem,
Because that studies spectacles and shows,   65
And after varied, as fresh objects, goes,
Giddy with change, and therefore cannot see
Right, the right way; yet must your comfort be
Your conscience, and not wonder if none asks
For truth's complexion, where they all wear masks.   70
Let who will follow fashions and attires,
Maintain their leigers forth for foreign wires,
Melt down their husbands' land, to pour away
On the close groom and page, on new-year's day,
And almost all days after, while they live;   75
They find it both so witty and safe to give.
Let them on powders, oils, and paintings spend,
Till that no usurer, nor his bawds dare lend

Them or their officers; and no man know,
Whether it be a face they wear or no.   80
Let them waste body and state; and after all,
When their own parasites laugh at their fall,
May they have nothing left whereof they can
Boast, but how oft they have gone wrong to man,
And call it their brave sin: for such there be   85
That do sin only for the infamy;
And never think how vice doth every hour
Eat on her clients, and some one devour.
You, madam, young have learned to shun these shelves,
Whereon the most of mankind wreck themselves,   90
And keeping a just course, have early put
Into your harbour, and all passage shut
'Gainst storms or pirates, that might charge your peace;
For which you worthy are the glad increase
Of your blest womb, made fruitful from above   95
To pay your lord the pledges of chaste love;
And raise a noble stem, to give the fame
To Clifton's blood, that is denied their name.
Grow, grow, fair tree! and as thy branches shoot,
Hear what the Muses sing about thy root,   100
By me, their priest, if they can aught divine:
Before the moons have filled their triple trine,
To crown the burden which you go withal,
It shall a ripe and timely issue fall,
T' expect the honours of great AUBIGNY;   105
And greater rites, yet writ in mystery,
But which the Fates forbid me to reveal.
Only thus much out of a ravished zeal
Unto your name, and goodness of your life,
They speak; since you are truly that rare wife   110
Other great wives may blush at, when they see
What your tried manners are, what theirs should be;
How you love one, and him you should, how still
You are depending on his word and will;
Not fashioned for the court, or strangers' eyes;   115
But to please him, who is the dearer prize
Unto himself, by being so dear to you.
This makes, that your affections still be new,
And that your souls conspire, as they were gone
Each into other, and had now made one.   120
Live that one still! and as long years do pass,
Madam, be bold to use this truest glass;
Wherein your form you still the same shall find;
Because nor it can change, nor such a mind.

A Celebration of Charis in ten lyric pieces (extract)

Her Triumph

See the chariot at hand here of love,
     Wherein my lady rideth!
Each that draws is a swan or a dove,
     And well the car love guideth.
As she goes all hearts do duty   5
          Unto her beauty,
And enamoured do wish so they might
          But enjoy such a sight,
That they still were to run by her side,
Through swords, through seas, whither she would ride.   10

Do but look on her eyes; they do light
     All that love's world compriseth!
Do but look on her hair; it is bright
     As love's star when it riseth!
Do but mark, her forehead's smoother   15
          Than words that soothe her:
And from her arched brows, such a grace
          Sheds itself through the face,
As alone there triumphs to the life
All the gain, all the good of the elements' strife.   20

Have you seen but a bright lily grow
     Before rude hands have touched it?
Ha' you marked but the fall o' the snow
     Before the soil hath smutched it?
Ha' you felt the wool of beaver,   25
          Or swan's down ever?
Or have smelt o' the bud o' the briar?
          Or the nard in the fire?
Or have tasted the bag of the bee?
O so white! O so soft! O so sweet is she!   30

My Picture, left in Scotland

I now think, Love is rather deaf than blind,
     For else it could not be,
          That she
     Whom I adore so much, should so slight me,
And cast my suit behind: 5
I'm sure my language to her was as sweet,

And every close did meet
In sentence of as subtle feet,
As hath the youngest he
That sits in shadow of Apollo's tree.   10

Oh! but my conscious fears,
        That fly my thoughts between,
Tell me that she hath seen
        My hundreds of gray hairs
                Told six and forty years,   15
    Read so much waste as she cannot embrace
    My mountain belly and my rocky face,
And all these, through her eyes, have stopt her ears.

An Epitaph on Master Vincent Corbet

I have my piety too, which, could
It vent itself but as it would,
Would say as much as both have done
Before me here, the friend and son:
For I both lost a friend and father,   5
Of him whose bones this grave doth gather,
Dear VINCENT CORBET, who so long
Had wrestled with diseases strong,
That though they did possess each limb,
Yet he broke them, ere they could him,   10
With the just canon of his life,
A life that knew nor noise nor strife;
But was, by sweetening so his will,
All order and disposure still.
    His mind as pure and neatly kept,   15
As were his nourceries, and swept
So of uncleanness or offence,
That never came ill odour thence!
And add his actions unto these,
They were as specious as his trees.   20
'Tis true, he could not reprehend—
His very manners taught t' amend,
They were so even, grave and holy;
No stubbornness so stiff, nor folly
To license ever was so light,   25
As twice to trespass in his sight:
His looks would so correct it, when
It child the vice yet not the men.
Much from him I profess I won,
And more and more I should have done,   30
But that I understood him scant.

Now I conceive him by my want;
And pray who shall my sorrows read,
That they for me their tears will shed;
For truly, since he left to be,   35
I feel I'm rather dead than he!
Reader, whose life and name did e'er become
    An Epitaph, deserved a Tomb:
Nor wants it here through penury or sloth,
    Who makes the one, so it be first, makes both.   40

To the Immortal Memory and Friendship of that Noble Pair, Sir Lucius Cary and Sir H. Morison

The Turn

Brave infant of Saguntum, clear
Thy coming forth in that great year
When the prodigious Hannibal did crown
His rage with razing your immortal town.
Thou, looking then about,   5
Ere thou wert half got out,
Wise child, didst hastily return
And mad'st thy mother's womb thine urn.
How summed a circle didst thou leave mankind,
Of deepest lore, could we the centre find!   10

The Counter-turn

Did wiser nature draw thee back
From out the horror of that sack,
Where shame, faith, honour, and regard of right
Lay trampled on? The deeds of death and night
Urged, hurried forth, and hurled   15
Upon the affrighted world;
Sword, fire, and famine with fell fury met,
And all on utmost ruin set;
As, could they but life's miseries foresee,
No doubt all infants would return like thee.   20

The Stand

For what is life, if measured by the space,
Not by the act?
Or masked man, if valued by his face,
Above his fact?
Here's one outlived his peers,   25
And told forth fourscore years;

He vexed time, and busied the whole state,
Troubled both foes and friends,
But ever to no ends;
What did this stirrer but die late? 30
How well at twenty had he fallen or stood!
For three of his fourscore he did no good.

The Turn

He entered well, by virtuous parts
Got up, and thrived with honest arts;
He purchased friends and fame, and honors then, 35
And had his noble name advanced with men.
But weary of that flight,
He stooped in all men's sight
To sordid flatteries, acts of strife,
And sunk in that dead sea of life 40
So deep as he did then death's waters sup,
But that the cork of title buoyed him up.

The Counter-turn

Alas, but Morison fell young!
He never fell,—thou fall'st, my tongue.
He stood, a soldier to the last right end, 45
A perfect patriot and a noble friend,
But most, a virtuous son.
All offices were done
By him so ample, full, and round,
In weight, in measure, number, sound, 50
As, though his age imperfect might appear,
His life was of humanity the sphere.

The Stand

Go now, and tell out days summed up with fears,
And make them years;
Produce thy mass of miseries on the stage, 55
To swell thine age;
Repeat of things a throng,
To show thou hast been long,
Not lived, for life doth her great actions spell
By what was done and wrought 60
In season, and so brought
To light; her measures are, how well
Each syllable answered, and was formed how fair;
These make the lines of life, and that's her air.

The Turn

It is not growing like a tree   65
In bulk. doth make man better be;
Or standing long an oak, three hundred year,
To fall a log at last, dry, bald, and sere;
A lily of a day
Is fairer far in May,   70
Although it fall and die that night,
It was the plant and flower of light.
In small proportions we just beauties see;
And in short measures, life may perfect be.

The Counter-turn

Call, noble Lucius, then for wine,   75
And let thy looks with gladness shine;
Accept this garland, plant it on thy head,
And think, nay know, thy Morison's not dead.
He leaped the present age,
Possessed with holy rage,   80
To see that bright eternal day
Of which we priests and poets say
Such truths as we expect for happy men,
And there he lives with memory, and Ben

The Stand

Jonson, who sung this of him, ere he went   85
Himself to rest,
Or taste a part of that full joy he meant
To have expressed
In this bright asterism,
Where it were friendship's schism,   90
Were not his Lucius long with us to tarry,
To separate these twi-
Lights, the Dioscuri,
And keep the one half from his Harry.
But fate doth so alternate the design,   95
Whilst that in heav'n, this light on earth must shine.

The Turn

And shine as you exalted are,
Two names of friendship, but one star;
Of hearts the union, and those not by chance
Made, or indenture, or leased out t' advance   100
The profits for a time.

No pleasures vain did chime
Of rhymes, or riots at your feasts,
Orgies of drink, or feigned protests;
But simple love of greatness and of good,   105
That knits brave minds and manners more than blood.

The Counter-turn

This made you first to know the why
You liked, then after to apply
That liking; and approach so one the t'other
Till either grew a portion of the other;   110
Each styled by his end
The copy of his friend.
You lived to be the great surnames
And titles by which all made claims
Unto the virtue; nothing perfect done   115
But as a Cary, or a Morison.

The Stand

And such a force the fair example had,
As they that saw
The good, and durst not practise it, were glad
That such a law   120
Was left yet to mankind,
Where they might read and find
Friendship in deed was written, not in words;
And with the heart, not pen,
Of two so early men,   125
Whose lines her rolls were, and records;
Who, ere the first down bloomed on the chin,
Had sowed these fruits, and got the harvest in.

An Elegy

On the Lady Jane Pawlet, Marchioness of Winton

What gentle ghost, besprent with April dew,
Hails me so solemnly to yonder yew,
And beckoning woos me, from the fatal tree
To pluck a garland for herself or me?
I do obey you, Beauty! for in death   5
You seem a fair one. O that you had breath
To give your shade a name! Stay, stay, I feel
A horror in me, all my blood is steel;
Stiff! stark! my joints 'gainst one another knock!
Whose daughter?—Ha! great Savage of the Rock.   10

He's good as great. I am almost a stone!
And ere I can ask more of her, she's gone!—
Alas, I am all marble! write the rest
Thou wouldst have written, Fame, upon my breast:
It is a large fair table, and a true,   15
And the disposure will be something new,
When I, who would the poet have become,
At least may bear the inscription to her tomb.
She was the Lady JANE, and Marchioness
Of Winchester; the heralds can tell this.   20
Earl Rivers' grandchild—'serve not forms, good Fame,
Sound thou her virtues, give her soul a name.
Had I a thousand mouths, as many tongues,
And voice to raise them from my brazen lungs,
I durst not aim at that; the dotes were such   25
Thereof, no notion can express how much
Their caract was: I or my trump must break,
But rather I, should I of that part speak;
It is too near of kin to heaven, the soul,
To be described! Fame's fingers are too foul   30
To touch these mysteries: we may admire
The heat and splendour, but not handle fire.
What she did here, by great example, well,
To enlive posterity, her Fame may tell;
And calling Truth to witness, make that good   35
From the inherent graces in her blood!
Else who doth praise a person by a new
But a feigned way, doth rob it of the true.
Her Sweetness, Softness, her fair Courtesy,
Her wary guards, her wise simplicity,   40
Were like a ring of Virtues 'bout her set,
And Piety the centre where all met.
A reverend state she had, an awful eye,
A dazzling, yet inviting, majesty:
What Nature, Fortune, Institution, Fact   45
Could sum to a perfection, was her Act!
How did she leave the world, with what contempt!
Just as she in it lived, and so exempt
From all affection! when they urged the cure
Of her disease, how did her soul assure   50
Her sufferings, as the body had been away!
And to the torturers, her doctors, say,
Stick on your cupping-glasses, fear not, put
Your hottest caustics to, burn, lance, or cut:
'Tis but a body which you can torment,   55
And I into the world all Soul was sent:
Then comforted her lord, and blest her son,
Cheered her fair sisters in her race to run,

With gladness tempered her sad parents tears,
Made her friends joys to get above their fears,   60
And in her last act taught the standers-by
With admiration and applause to die!
    Let Angels sing her glories, who did call
Her spirit home to her original;
Who saw the way was made it, and were sent   65
To carry and conduct the complement
'Twixt death and life, where her mortality
Became her birth-day to eternity!
And now through circumfused light she looks,
On Nature's secret there, as her own books: 70
Speaks heaven's language, and discourseth free
To every order, every hierarchy!
Beholds her Maker, and in him doth see
What the beginnings of all beauties be;
And all beatitudes that thence do flow: 75
Which they that have the crown are sure to know!
    Go now, her happy parents, and be sad,
If you not understand what child you had.
If you dare grudge at heaven, and repent
To have paid again a blessing was but lent,   80
And trusted so, as it deposited lay
At pleasure, to be called for every day!
If you can envy your own daughter's bliss,
And wish her state less happy than it is;
If you can cast about your either eye,   85
And see all dead here, or about to die!
The stars, that are the jewels of the night,
And day, deceasing, with the prince of light,
The sun, great kings, and mightiest kingdoms fall;
Whole nations, nay, mankind! the world, with all   90
That ever had beginning there, t' have end!
With what injustice should one soul pretend
To escape this common known necessity?
When we were all born, we began to die;
And, but for that contention, and brave strife   95
The Christian hath to enjoy the future life,
He were the wretched'st of the race of men:
But as he soars at that, he bruiseth then
The serpent's head; gets above death and sin,
And, sure of heaven, rides triumphing in.   100

From *Cynthia's Revels*

[*Slow, slow, fresh fount*]

Slow, slow, fresh fount, keep time with my salt tears;
  Yet slower yet, oh faintly, gentle springs;
List to the heavy part the music bears,
    Woe weeps out her division when she sings.
      Droop herbs and flowers,   5
      Fall grief in showers;
      Our beauties are not ours;
        Oh, I could still,
Like melting snow upon some craggy hill,
  Drop, drop, drop, drop,   10
Since nature's pride is now a withered daffodil.

Robert Herrick
(1591–1674)

From *Hesperides*

The Argument of his Book

I sing of brooks, of blossoms, birds, and bowers,
Of April, May, of June, and July flowers;
I sing of may-poles, hock-carts, wassails, wakes,
Of bridegrooms, brides, and of their bridal cakes;
I write of youth, of love, and have access 5
By these to sing of cleanly wantonness;
I sing of dews, of rains, and piece by piece
Of balm, of oil, of spice, and ambergris;
I sing of times trans-shifting, and I write
How roses first came red, and lilies white; 10
I write of groves, of twilights, and I sing
The court of Mab, and of the Fairy King;
I write of hell; I sing, and ever shall,
Of heaven, and hope to have it after all.

When he would have his Verses Read

In sober mornings do not thou rehearse
The holy incantation of a verse;
But when that men have both well drunk and fed,
Let my enchantments then be sung, or read.
When laurel spirts i' th' fire, and when the hearth 5
Smiles to itself and gilds the roof with mirth;
When up the thyrse is raised, and when the sound
Of sacred orgies flies—A round, a round!
When the rose reigns, and locks with ointments shine,
Let rigid Cato read these lines of mine. 10

Delight in Disorder

A sweet disorder in the dress
Kindles in clothes a wantonness;

A lawn about the shoulders thrown
Into a fine distraction,
An erring lace, which here and there   5
Enthralls the crimson stomacher,
A cuff neglectful, and thereby
Ribands to flow confusedly,
A winning wave, deserving note,
In the tempestuous petticoat,   10
A careless shoe-string, in whose tie
I see a wild civility,
Do more bewitch me than when art
Is too precise in every part.

To the Virgins, to Make Much of Time

Gather ye rosebuds while ye may,
    Old time is still a-flying,
And this same flower that smiles today,
    Tomorrow will be dying.

The glorious lamp of heaven, the sun,   5
    The higher he's a-getting,
The sooner will his race be run,
    And nearer he's to setting.

That age is best which is the first,
    When youth and blood are warmer;   10
But being spent, the worse, and worst
    Times still succeed the former.

Then be not coy, but use your time,
    And while ye may, go marry;
For having lost but once your prime,   15
    You may for ever tarry.

Upon Julia's Clothes

Whenas in silks my Julia goes,
Then, then, methinks, how sweetly flows
That liquefaction of her clothes.
Next, when I cast mine eyes and see
That brave vibration each way free,   5
Oh, how that glittering taketh me!

The Funeral Rites of the Rose

The Rose was sick and smiling died;
And, being to be sanctified,
About the bed there sighing stood
The sweet and flowery sisterhood:
Some hung the head, while some did bring,   5
To wash her, water from the spring;
Some laid her forth, while others wept,
But all a solemn fast there kept:
The holy sisters, some among,
The sacred dirge and trental sung.   10
But ah! what sweets smelt everywhere,
As Heaven had spent all perfumes there.
At last, when prayers for the dead
And rites were all accomplishéd,
They, weeping, spread a lawny loom,   15
And closed her up as in a tomb.

To Daisies, not to shut so soon

Shut not so soon; the dull-eyed nigh
    Has not as yet begun
To make a seizure on the light,
    Or to seal up the sun.

No marigolds yet closed are,   5
    No shadows great appear;
Nor doth the early shepherd's star
    Shine like a spangle here.

Stay but till my Julia close
    Her life-begetting eye,   10
And let the whole world then dispose
    Itself to live or die.

Cherry-Ripe

Cherry-ripe, ripe, ripe, I cry,
Full and fair ones; come and buy.
If so be you ask me where
They do grow, I answer: There,
Where my Julia's lips do smile;   5
There's the land, or cherry-isle,
Whose plantations fully show
All the year where cherries grow.

His Cavalier

Give me that man that dares bestride
The active sea-horse, and with pride
Through that huge field of waters ride;
Who with his looks too can appease
The ruffling winds and raging seas   5
In midst of all their outrages.
This, this a virtuous man can do:
Sail against rocks and split them too;
Ay, and a world of pikes pass through.

The Difference betwixt Kings and Subjects

'Twixt kings and subjects there's this mighty odds,
Subjects are taught by men; kings by the gods.

Kings and Tyrants

'Twixt kings and tyrants there's this difference known,
Kings seek their subjects' good; tyrants their own.

Slavery

'Tis liberty to serve one lord, but he
Who many serves, serves base servility.

Ill Government

Preposterous is that government, and rude,
When kings obey the wilder multitude.

His Return to London

From the dull confines of the drooping west
To see the day spring from the pregnant east,
Ravished in spirit, I come, nay more, I fly
To thee, blest place of my nativity!
Thus, thus with hallowed foot I touch the ground   5
With thousand blessings by thy fortune crowned.
O fruitful genius! that bestowest here

An everlasting plenty, year by year.
O place! O people! Manners framed to please
All nations, customs, kindreds, languages!   10
I am a free-born Roman, suffer then
That I amongst you live a citizen.
London my home is, though by hard fate sent
Into a long and irksome banishment;
Yet since called back, henceforward let me be,   15
O native country, repossessed by thee!
For rather than I'll to the west return,
I'll beg of thee first here to have mine run.
Weak I am grown, and must in short time fall;
Give thou my sacred relics burial.   20

Henry King
(1592–1669)

The Exequy

Accept, thou shrine of my dead saint,
Instead of dirges, this complaint;
And for sweet flowers to crown thy hearse,
Receive a strew of weeping verse
From thy grieved friend, whom thou might'st see   5
Quite melted into tears for thee.

Dear loss! since thy untimely fate
My task hath been to meditate
On thee, on thee; thou art the book,
The library whereon I look,   10
Though almost blind. For thee, loved clay,
I languish out, not live, the day,
Using no other exercise
But what I practise with mine eyes:
By which wet glasses I find out   15
How lazily time creeps about
To one that mourns; this, only this,
My exercise and business is.
So I compute the weary hours
With sighs dissolved into showers.   20

Nor wonder if my time go thus
Backward and most preposterous;
Thou hast benighted me; thy set
This eve of blackness did beget,
Who wast my day, though overcast   25
Before thou hadst thy noontide passed;
And I remember must in tears,
Thou scarce hadst seen so many years
As day tells hours. By thy clear sun
My love and fortune first did run;   30
But thou wilt never more appear
Folded within my hemisphere,
Since both thy light and motion
Like a fled star is fallen and gone;

And 'twixt me and my soul's dear wish   35
An earth now interposed is,
Which such a strange eclipse doth make
As ne'er was read in almanac.

I could allow thee for a time
To darken me and my sad clime;   40
Were it a month, a year, or ten,
I would thy exile live till then,
And all that space my mirth adjourn,
So thou wouldst promise to return,
And putting off thy ashy shroud,   45
At length disperse this sorrow's cloud.

But woe is me! the longest date
Too narrow is to calculate
These empty hopes; never shall I
Be so much blest as to descry   50
A glimpse of thee, till that day come
Which shall the earth to cinders doom,
And a fierce fever must calcine
The body of this world like thine,
My little world. That fit of fire   55
Once off, our bodies shall aspire
To our souls' bliss; then we shall rise
And view ourselves with clearer eyes
In that calm region where no night
Can hide us from each other's sight.   60

Meantime, thou hast her, earth; much good
May my harm do thee. Since it stood
With heaven's will I might not call
Her longer mine, I give thee all
My short-lived right and interest   65
In her whom living I loved best;
With a most free and bounteous grief,
I give thee what I could not keep.
Be kind to her, and prithee look
Thou write into thy doomsday book   70
Each parcel of this rarity
Which in thy casket shrined doth lie.
See that thou make thy reck'ning straight,
And yield her back again by weight;
For thou must audit on thy trust   75
Each grain and atom of this dust,
As thou wilt answer Him that lent,
Not gave thee, my dear monument.

So close the ground, and 'bout her shade
Black curtains draw, my bride is laid.   80

Sleep on, my love, in thy cold bed,
Never to be disquieted!
My last good-night! Thou wilt not wake
Till I thy fate shall overtake;
Till age, or grief, or sickness must   85
Marry my body to that dust
It so much loves, and fill the room
My heart keeps empty in thy tomb.
Stay for me there, I will not fail
To meet thee in that hollow vale.   90
And think not much of my delay;
I am already on the way,
And follow thee with all the speed
Desire can make, or sorrows breed.
Each minute is a short degree,   95
And every hour a step towards thee.
At night when I betake to rest,
Next morn I rise nearer my west
Of life, almost by eight hours' sail,
Than when sleep breathed his drowsy gale.   100

Thus from the sun my bottom steers,
And my day's compass downward bears;
Nor labour I to stem the tide
Through which to thee I swiftly glide.

'Tis true, with shame and grief I yield,   105
Thou like the van first tookst the field,
And gotten hath the victory
In thus adventuring to die
Before me, whose more years might crave
A just precedence in the grave.   110
But hark! my pulse like a soft drum
Beats my approach, tells thee I come;
And slow howe'er my marches be,
I shall at last sit down by thee.

The thought of this bids me go on,   115
And wait my dissolution
With hope and comfort. Dear, forgive
The crime, I am content to live
Divided, with but half a heart,
Till we shall meet and never part.   120

George Herbert
(1593–1633)

The Pulley

When God at first made man,
Having a glass of blessings standing by;
Let us (said he) pour on him all we can:
Let the world's riches, which dispersed lie,
    Contract into a span.   5

So strength first made a way;
Then beauty flow'd, then wisdom, honour, pleasure:
When almost all was out, God made a stay,
Perceiving that alone, of all his treasure,
    Rest in the bottom lay.   10

For if I should (said he)
Bestow this jewel also on my creature,
He would adore my gifts instead of me,
And rest in Nature, not the God of Nature:
    So both should losers be.   15

Yet let him keep the rest,
But keep them with repining restlessness:
Let him be rich and weary, that at least,
If goodness lead him not, yet weariness
    May toss him to my breast.   20

Church Monuments

While that my soul repairs to her devotion,
Here I entomb my flesh, that it betimes
May take acquaintance of this heap of dust;
To which the blast of death's incessant motion,
Fed with the exhalation of our crimes,   5
Drives all at last. Therefore I gladly trust

My body to this school, that it may learn
To spell his elements, and find his birth

Written in dusty heraldry and lines;
Which dissolution sure doth best discern,   10
Comparing dust with dust, and earth with earth.
These laugh at Jet, and Marble put for signs,

To sever the good fellowship of dust,
And spoil the meeting. What shall point out them,
When they shall bow, and kneel, and fall down flat   15
To kiss those heaps, which now they have in trust?
Dear flesh, while I do pray, learn here thy stem
And true descent; that when thou shalt grow fat,

And wanton in thy cravings, thou may'st know,
That flesh is but the glass, which holds the dust   20
That measures all our time; which also shall
Be crumbled into dust. Mark here below,
How tame these ashes are, how free from lust,
That thou may'st fit thyself against thy fall.

Redemption

Having been tenant long to a rich Lord,
      Not thriving, I resolved to be bold,
      And make a suit unto him, to afford
A new small-rented lease, and cancel the old.

In Heaven at his manor I him sought: 5
      They told me there, that he was lately gone
      About some land, which he had dearly bought
Long since on earth, to take possession.

I straight returned, and knowing his great birth,
      Sought him accordingly in great resorts;   10
      In cities, theatres, gardens, parks, and courts:
At length I heard a ragged noise and mirth

      Of thieves and murderers: there I him espied,
      Who straight, *Your suit is granted*, said, and died.

Nature

Full of rebellion, I would die,
Or fight, or travel, or deny
That thou hast aught to do with me.
            O tame my heart;
            It is thy highest art   5
To captivate strong holds to thee.

If thou shalt let this venom lurk,
And in suggestions fume and work,
My soul will turn to bubbles straight,
               And thence by kind   10
             Vanish into a wind,
Making thy workmanship deceit.

O smooth my rugged heart and there
Engrave thy reverend law and fear;
Or make a new one, since the old   15
              Is sapless grown,
              And a much fitter stone
To hide my dust, than thee to hold.

Prayer

Prayer the Church's banquet, angels' age,
   God's breath in man returning to his birth,
   The soul in paraphrase, heart in pilgrimage,
The Christian plummet sounding heaven and earth;
Engine against the Almighty, sinner's tower,   5
   Reversed thunder, Christ-side-piercing spear,
   The six-days-world transposing in an hour,
A kind of tune, which all things hear and fear;
Softness, and peace, and joy, and love, and bliss,
   Exalted manna, gladness of the best,   10
   Heaven in ordinary, man well-dressed,
The Milky Way, the bird of paradise,
   Church-bells beyond the stars heard, the soul's blood,
   The land of spices; something understood.

The Pilgrimage

I travelled on, seeing the hill, where lay
      My expectation.
   A long it was and weary way.
   The gloomy cave of Desperation
I left on the one, and on the other side   5
      The rock of Pride.

And so I came to Fancy's meadow strewed
      With many a flower:
   Fain would I here have made abode,
   But I was quickened by the hour.   10
So to Care's copse I came, and there got through
      With much ado.

That led me to the wild of Passion; which
        Some call the wold;
    A wasted place, but sometimes rich.   15
    Here I was robbed of all my gold,
Save one good angel, which a friend had tied
        Close to my side.

At length I got unto the gladsome hill,
        Where lay my hope,   20
    Where lay my heart; and climbing still,
    When I had gained the brow and top,
A lake of brackish waters on the ground
        Was all I found.

With that abashed and struck with many a sting   25
        Of swarming fears,
    I fell, and cried, Alas! my King;
    Can both the way and end be tears?
Yet taking heart I rose, and then perceived
        I was deceived: 30

My hill was further: so I flung away,
        Yet heard a cry
    Just as I went, *None goes that way*
    And lives: If that be all, said I,
After so foul a journey death is fair,   35
        And but a chair.

Artillery

As I one evening sat before my cell,
Methoughts a star did shoot into my lap.
I rose and shook my clothes, as knowing well
That from small fires comes oft no small mishap –
    When suddenly I heard one say,   5
    "Do as thou usest, disobey,
    Expel good motions from thy breast,
Which have the face of fire, but end in rest."

I, who had heard of music in the spheres
But not of speech in stars, began to muse   10
But turning to my God, whose ministers
The stars and all things are; "If I refuse,
    Dread Lord," said I, "so oft my good;
    Then I refuse not even with blood
    To wash away my stubborn thought: 15
For I will do, or suffer what I ought.

But I have also stars and shooters too,
Born where thy servants both artilleries use.
My tears and prayers night and day do woo
And work up to thee; yet thou dost refuse.   20
   Nor, but I am (I must say still)
   Much more obliged to do thy will,
   Than thou to grant mine: but because
Thy promise now hath even set thee thy laws.

Then we are shooters both, and thou dost deign   25
To enter combat with us, and contest
With thine own clay. But I would parley fain:
Shun not my arrows, and behold my breast.
   Yet if thou shunnest, I am thine:
   I must be so, if I am mine.   30
   There is no articling with thee:
I am but finite, yet thine infinitely."

The Collar

   I struck the board, and cried, "No more,
      I will abroad.
   What? shall I ever sigh and pine?
My lines and life are free; free as the road,
   Loose as the wind, as large as store.   5
      Shall I be still in suit?
   Have I no harvest but a thorn
   To let me blood, and not restore
What I have lost with cordial fruit?
      Sure there was wine   10
Before my sighs did dry it: there was corn
      Before my tears did drown it.
   Is the year only lost to me?
      Have I no bays to crown it?
No flowers, no garlands gay? all blasted?   15
      All wasted?
   Not so, my heart: but there is fruit,
      And thou hast hands.
   Recover all thy sigh-blown age
On double pleasures: leave thy cold dispute   20
Of what is fit, and not. Forsake thy cage,
      Thy rope of sands
Which petty thoughts have made, and made to thee
   Good cable, to enforce and draw
      And be thy law,   25
   While thou didst wink and wouldst not see.
      Away; take heed:

I will abroad.
Call in thy death's head there: tie up thy fears.
          He that forbears   30
      To suit and serve his need
          Deserves his load."
But as I raved and grew more fierce and wild
          At every word
Methoughts I heard one calling, "Child":   35
          And I replied, "My Lord."

The Flower

How fresh, O Lord, how sweet and clean
Are thy returns! even as the flowers in spring –
    To which, besides their own demesne,
The late-past frosts tributes of pleasure bring.
          Grief melts away   5
          Like snow in May
    As if there were no such cold thing.

Who would have thought my shrivelled heart
Could have recovered greenness? It was gone
          Quite underground; as flowers depart   10
To see their mother-root when they have blown;
          Where they together
          All the hard weather,
    Dead to the world, keep house unknown.

These are thy wonders, Lord of Power,   15
Killing and quickening, bringing down to Hell
    And up to Heaven in an hour,
Making a chiming of a passing-bell;
          We say amiss,
          This or that is: 20
    Thy Word is all, if we could spell.

O that I once past chaning were,
Fast in thy Paradise, where no flower can wither!
    Many a spring I shoot up fair,
Offering at heaven, growing and groaning thither: 25
          Nor doth my flower
          Want a spring shower,
    My sins and I joining together:

But while I grow in a straight line,
Still upwards bent, as if heaven were mine own,   30
    Thy anger comes, and I decline:

What frost to that? what pole is not the zone,
        Where all things burn,
        When thou dost turn,
And the least frown of thine is shown?   35

    And now in age I bud again,
After so many deaths I live and write;
   I once more smell the dew and rain,
And relish versing: O my only light,
        It cannot be   40
        That I am he
On whom thy tempests fell all night.

    These are thy wonders, Lord of Love,
To make us see we are but flowers that glide,
   Which when we once can find and prove,   45
Thou hast a garden for us, where to bide.
        Who would be more,
        Swelling through store,
Forfeit their Paradise by their pride.

Love

Love bade me welcome: yet my soul drew back,
    Guilty of dust and sin.
But quick-eyed Love, observing me grow slack
    From my first entrance in,
Drew nearer to me, sweetly questioning,   5
    If I lacked any thing.

"A guest", I answered, worthy to be here:
    Love said, "You shall be he."
"I the unkind, ungrateful? Ah, my dear,
    I cannot look on thee."   10
Love took my hand, and smiling did reply,
    "Who made the eyes but I?"

"Truth Lord, but I have marred them: let my shame
    Go where it doth deserve."
"And know you not", says Love, "who bore the blame?"   15
    "My dear, then I will serve."
"You must sit down", says Love, "and taste my meat":
    So I did sit and eat.

John Milton
(1608–1674)

L'Allegro

Hence, loathed Melancholy,
Of Cerberus and blackest Midnight born,
In Stygian cave forlorn,
   'Mongst horrid shapes, and shrieks, and sights unholy!
Find out some uncouth cell,   5
   Where brooding Darkness spreads his jealous wings,
   And the night-raven sings;
There under ebon shades and low-browed rocks,
As ragged as thy locks,
   In dark Cimmerian desert ever dwell.   10
   But come, thou goddess fair and free,
In Heaven ycleped Euphrosyne,
And by men, heart-easing Mirth;
Whom lovely Venus, at a birth,
With two sister Graces more,   15
To ivy-crowned Bacchus bore:
Or whether (as some sager sing)
The frolic wind that breathes the spring,
Zephyr, with Aurora playing,
As he met her once a-Maying;   20
There on beds of violets blue,
And fresh-blown roses washed in dew,
Filled her with thee a daughter fair,
So buxom, blithe, and debonair.
   Haste thee, nymph, and bring with thee   25
Jest, and youthful jollity,
Quips, and cranks, and wanton wiles,
Nods, and becks, and wreathed smiles,
Such as hang on Hebe's cheek,
And love to live in dimples sleek;   30
Sport that wrinkled Care derides,
And Laughter holding both his sides.
Come, and trip it, as you go,
On the light fantastic toe;
And in thy right hand lead with thee   35
The mountain-nymph sweet Liberty;

And, if I give thee honour due,
Mirth, admit me of thy crew,
To live with her, and live with thee,
In unreproved pleasures free;   40
To hear the lark begin his flight,
And singing startle the dull night,
From his watchtower in the skies,
Till the dappled dawn doth rise;
Then to come, in spite of sorrow,   45
And at my window bid good morrow,
Through the sweetbriar, or the vine,
Or the twisted eglantine:
While the cock, with lively din,
Scatters the rear of darkness thin;   50
And to the stack, or the barn-door,
Stoutly struts his dame before:
Oft listening how the hounds and horn
Cheerly rouse the slumbering morn,
From the side of some hoar hill,   55
Through the high wood echoing shrill:
Some time walking, not unseen,
By hedgerow elms, on hillocks green,
Right against the eastern gate
Where the great sun begins his state,   60
Robed in flames, and amber light
The clouds in thousand liveries dight;
While the ploughman, near at hand,
Whistles o'er the furrowed land,
And the milkmaid singeth blithe,   65
And the mower whets his scythe,
And every shepherd tells his tale
Under the hawthorn in the dale.
Straight mine eye hath caught new pleasures,
Whilst the landskip round it measures;   70
Russet lawns, and fallows gray,
Where the nibbling flocks do stray;
Mountains, on whose barren breast
The labouring clouds do often rest;
Meadows trim with daisies pied,   75
Shallow brooks, and rivers wide:
Towers and battlements it sees
Bosomed high in tufted trees,
Where perhaps some Beauty lies,
The cynosure of neighbouring eyes.   80
Hard by, a cottage chimney smokes,
From betwixt two aged oaks,
Where Corydon and Thyrsis, met,
Are at their savoury dinner set

Of herbs, and other country messes,   85
Which the neat-handed Phillis dresses;
And then in haste her bower she leaves,
With Thestylis to bind the sheaves;
Or, if the earlier season lead,
To the tanned haycock in the mead.   90
    Sometimes with secure delight
The upland hamlets will invite,
When the merry bells ring round,
And the jocund rebecks sound
To many a youth, and many a maid,   95
Dancing in the chequered shade;
And young and old come forth to play
On a sunshine holy-day,
Till the livelong daylight fail:
Then to the spicy nut-brown ale,   100
With stories told of many a feat,
How fairy Mab the junkets eat;
She was pinched, and pulled, she said;
And he, by friar's lantern led,
Tells how the drudging Goblin sweat.   105
To earn his cream-bowl duly set,
When in one night, ere glimpse of morn,
His shadowy flail hath threshed the corn,
That ten day-labourers could not end;
Then lies him down the lubbar fiend,   110
And, stretched out all the chimney's length,
Basks at the fire his hairy strength;
And crop-full out of doors he flings,
Ere the first cock his matin rings.
Thus done the tales, to bed they creep,   115
By whispering winds soon lulled asleep.
Towered cities please us then,
And the busy hum of men,
Where throngs of knights and barons bold,
In weeds of peace, high triumphs hold,   120
With store of ladies, whose bright eyes
Rain influence, and judge the prize
Of wit or arms, while both contend
To win her grace, whom all commend.
There let Hymen oft appear   125
In saffron robe, with taper clear,
And pomp, and feast, and revelry,
With mask, and antique pageantry;
Such sights as youthful poets dream
On summer eves by haunted stream.   130
Then to the well-trod stage anon,
If Jonson's learned sock be on,

Or sweetest Shakespeare, Fancy's child,
Warble his native woodnotes wild.
   And ever, against eating cares,   135
Lap me in soft Lydian airs,
Married to immortal verse;
Such as the meeting soul may pierce,
In notes, with many a winding bout
Of linked sweetness long drawn out,   140
With wanton heed and giddy cunning;
The melting voice through mazes running,
Untwisting all the chains that tie
The hidden soul of harmony;
That Orpheus' self may heave his head   145
From golden slumber on a bed
Of heaped Elysian flowers, and hear
Such strains as would have won the ear
Of Pluto, to have quite set free
His half-regained Eurydice.   150
   These delights if thou canst give,
Mirth, with thee I mean to live.

Il Penseroso

Hence, vain deluding Joys,
   The brood of Folly without father bred!
   How little you bested,
Or fill the fixed mind with all your toys!
Dwell in some idle brain,   5
   And fancies fond with gaudy shapes possess,
   As thick and numberless
   As the gay motes that people the sunbeams;
   Or likest hovering dreams,
The fickle pensioners of Morpheus' train.   10
But hail, thou goddess, sage and holy,
Hail, divinest Melancholy!
Whose saintly visage is too bright
To hit the sense of human sight,
And therefore to our weaker view   15
O'erlaid with black, staid Wisdom's hue;
Black, but such as in esteem
Prince Memnon's sister might beseem,
Or that stared Ethiop queen that strove
To set her beauty's praise above   20
The sea-nymphs, and their powers offended:
Yet thou art higher far descended:
Thee, bright-haired Vesta, long of yore,
The solitary Saturn bore

His daughter she; in Saturn's reign,   25
Such mixture was not held a stain:
Oft in glimmering bowers and glades
He met her, and in secret shades
Of woody Ida's inmost grove,
Whilst yet there was no fear of Jove.   30
Come, pensive nun, devout and pure,
Sober, steadfast, and demure,
All in a robe of darkest grain,
Flowing with majestic train,
And sable stole of cyprus lawn,   35
Over thy decent shoulders drawn.
Come, but keep thy wonted state,
With even step, and musing gait;
And looks commercing with the skies,
Thy rapt soul sitting in thine eyes: 40
There, held in holy passion still,
Forget thyself to marble, till
With a sad leaden downward cast
Thou fix them on the earth as fast:
And join with thee calm Peace and Quiet,   45
Spare Fast, that oft with gods doth diet,
And hears the Muses in a ring
Aye round about Jove's altar sing:
And add to these retired Leisure,
That in trim gardens takes his pleasure: 50
But first, and chiefest, with thee bring,
Him that you soars on golden wing,
Guiding the fiery-wheeled throne,
The cherub Contemplation;
And the mute Silence hist along,   55
'Less Philomel will deign a song,
In her sweetest saddest plight,
Smoothing the rugged brow of night,
While Cynthia checks her dragon yoke,
Gently o'er the accustomed oak: 60
Sweet bird, that shun'st the noise of folly,
Most musical, most melancholy!
Thee, chauntress, oft, the woods among,
I woo, to hear thy evensong;
And, missing thee, I walk unseen   65
On the dry smooth-shaven green
To behold the wandering moon,
Riding near her highest noon,
Like one that had been led astray
Through the heaven's wide pathless way;   70
And oft, as if her head she bowed,
Stooping through a fleecy cloud.

Oft, on a plat of rising ground,
I hear the far-off curfew sound,
Over some wide-watered shore,   75
Swinging slow with sullen roar:
Or if the air will not permit
Some still removed place will fit,
Where glowing embers through the room
Teach light to counterfeit a gloom;   80
Far from all resort of mirth,
Save the cricket on the hearth,
Or the bellman's drowsy charm,
To bless the doors from nightly harm.
Or let my lamp, at midnight hour,   85
Be seen in some high lonely tower,
Where I may oft outwatch the Bear,
With thrice great Hermes, or unsphere
The spirit of Plato, to unfold
What worlds or what vast regions hold   90
The immortal mind that hath forsook
Her mansion in this fleshly nook:
And of those demons that are found
In fire, air, flood, or under ground,
Whose power hath a true consent   95
With planet, or with element.
Sometime let gorgeous Tragedy
In sceptred pall come sweeping by,
Presenting Thebes, or Pelops' line,
Or the tale of Troy divine;   100
Or what (though rare) of later age
Ennobled hath the buskined stage.
   But, O sad Virgin, that thy power
Might raise Musaeus from his bower!
Or bid the soul of Orpheus sing   105
Such notes, as, warbled to the string,
Drew iron tears down Pluto's cheek,
And made Hell grant what love did seek!
Or call up him that left half-told
The story of Cambuscan bold,   110
Of Camball, and of Algarsife,
And who had Canace to wife,
That owned the virtuous ring and glass;
And of the wondrous horse of brass
On which the Tartar king did ride: 115
And if aught else great bards beside
In sage and solemn tunes have sung,
Of turneys, and of trophies hung
Of forests, and enchantments drear,
Where more is meant than meets the ear.   120

Thus, Night, oft see me in thy pale career
Till civil-suited Morn appear;
Not tricked and frounced as she was wont
With the Attic boy to hunt,
But kercheft in a comely cloud,   125
While rocking winds are piping loud,
Or ushered with a shower still,
When the gust hath blown his fill,
Ending on the rustling leaves,
With minute drops from off the eaves.   130
And, when the sun begins to fling
His flaring beams, me, goddess, bring
To arched walks of twilight groves,
And shadows brown, that Sylvan loves,
Of pine, or monumental oak,   135
Where the rude axe, with heaved stroke,
Was never heard the nymphs to daunt,
Or fright them from their hallowed haunt.
There in close covert by some brook,
Where no profaner eye may look,   140
Hide me from day's garish eye,
While the bee with honied thigh,
That at her flowery work doth sing,
And the waters murmuring,
With such consort as they keep,   145
Entice the dewy-feathered Sleep;
And let some strange mysterious Dream
Wave at his wings in aery stream
Of lively portraiture displayed,
Softly on my eyelids laid.   150
And, as I wake, sweet music breathe
Above, about, or underneath,
Sent by some spirit to mortals good,
Or the unseen genius of the wood.
    But let my due feet never fail   155
To walk the studious cloisters pale,
And love the high-embowed roof,
With antic pillars massy proof,
And storied windows richly dight,
Casting a dim religious light: 160
There let the pealing organ blow,
To the full-voiced choir below,
In service high and anthems clear,
As may with sweetness, through mine ear,
Dissolve me into ecstasies,   165
And bring all heaven before mine eyes.
    And may at last my weary age
Find out the peaceful hermitage,

The hairy gown and mossy cell,
Where I may sit and rightly spell   170
Of every star that heaven doth show,
And every herb that sips the dew;
Till old experience do attain
To something like prophetic strain.
   These pleasures, Melancholy, give,   175
And I with thee will choose to live.

Lycidas

A Monody

In this Monody, the Author bewails a learned Friend, unfortunately drowned in his passage from Chester on the Irish Seas, 1637. And by occasion foretells the ruin of our corrupted clergy, then in their highth.

Yet once more, O ye laurels, and once more
Ye myrtles brown, with ivy never-sere,
I come to pluck your berries harsh and crude;
And, with forced fingers rude,
Shatter your leaves before the mellowing year: 5
Bitter constraint, and sad occasion dear,
Compels me to disturb your season due:
For Lycidas is dead, dead ere his prime,
Young Lycidas, and hath not left his peer:
Who would not sing for Lycidas?   He knew   10
Himself to sing, and build the lofty rhyme.
He must not float upon his watery bier
Unwept, and welter to the parching wind,
Without the meed of some melodious tear.
   Begin then, sisters of the sacred well,   15
That from beneath the seat of Jove doth spring;
Begin, and somewhat loudly sweep the string.
Hence with denial vain, and coy excuse:
So may some gentle Muse
With lucky words favour my destined urn;   20
And, as he passes, turn,
And bid fair peace be to my sable shroud.
   For we were nursed upon the self-same hill,
Fed the same flock by fountain, shade, and rill.
Together both, ere the high lawns appeared   25
Under the opening eyelids of the morn,
We drove a field, and both together heard
What time the gray-fly winds her sultry horn,
Battening our flocks with the fresh dews of night,
Oft, till the star, that rose, at evening, bright,   30

Toward heaven's descent had sloped his westering wheel.
Mean while the rural ditties were not mute,
Tempered to the oaten flute;
Rough satyrs danced, and fauns with cloven heel
From the glad sound would not be absent long;　　　　35
And old Damoetas loved to hear our song.
　　But, O the heavy change, now thou art gone,
Now thou art gone, and never must return!
Thee, shepherd, thee the woods, and desert caves
With wild thyme and the gadding vine o'ergrown,　　40
And all their echoes mourn:
The willows, and the hazel copses green,
Shall now no more be seen
Fanning their joyous leaves to thy soft lays.
As killing as the canker to the rose,　　　　　　　45
Or taint-worm to the weanling herds that graze,
Or frost to flowers, that their gay wardrobe wear,
When first the white-thorn blows;
Such, Lycidas, thy loss to shepherd's ear.
　　Where were ye, nymphs, when the remorseless deep　50
Closed o'er the head of your loved Lycidas?
For neither were ye playing on the steep,
Where your old bards, the famous Druids, lie,
Nor on the shaggy top of Mona high,
Nor yet where Deva spreads her wizard stream;　　55
Ay me, I fondly dream!
Had ye been there—for what could they have done?
What could the Muse herself that Orpheus bore,
The Muse herself, for her enchanting son,
Whom universal Nature did lament,　　　　　　60
When, by the rout that made the hideous roar,
His gory visage down the stream was sent,
Down the swift Hebrus to the Lesbian shore?
　　Alas! what boots it with incessant care
To tend the homely, slighted shepherd's trade,　　65
And strictly meditate the thankless Muse?
Were it not better done, as others use,
To sport with Amaryllis in the shade,
Or with the tangles of Neaera's hair?
Fame is the spur that the clear spirit doth raise　　70
(That last infirmity of noble mind)
To scorn delights, and live laborious days;
But the fair guerdon when we hope to find,
And think to burst out into sudden blaze,
Comes the blind Fury with the abhorred shears,　　75
And slits the thin-spun life. "But not the praise",
Phoebus replied, and touched my trembling ears;
"Fame is no plant that grows on mortal soil,

Nor in the glistering foil
Set off to the world, nor in broad rumour lies;   80
But lives and spreads aloft by those pure eyes,
And perfect witness of all-judging Jove;
As he pronounces lastly on each deed,
Of so much fame in heaven expect thy meed."
    O fountain Arethuse, and thou honoured flood,   85
Smooth-sliding Mincius, crowned with vocal reeds.
That strain I heard was of a higher mood:
But now my oat proceeds,
And listens to the herald of the sea
That came in Neptune's plea;   90
He asked the waves, and asked the felon winds,
What hard mishap hath doomed this gentle swain?
And questioned every gust of rugged wings
That blows from off each beaked promontory:
They knew not of his story;   95
And sage Hippotades their answer brings,
That not a blast was from his dungeon strayed;
The air was calm, and on the level brine
Sleek Panope with all her sisters played.
It was that fatal and perfidious bark,   100
Built in the eclipse, and rigged with curses dark,
That sunk so low that sacred head of thine.
    Next Camus, reverend sire, went footing slow,
His mantle hairy, and his bonnet sedge,
In wrought with figures dim, and on the edge   105
Like to that sanguine flower inscribed with woe.
"Ah! Who hath reft (quoth he) my dearest pledge?"
Last came, and last did go,
The pilot of the Galilean lake;
Two massy keys he bore of metals twain   110
(The golden opes, the iron shuts amain),
He shook his mitred locks, and stern bespake:
"How well could I have spared for thee, young swain,
Enow of such, as for their bellies' sake
Creep, and intrude, and climb into the fold?   115
Of other care they little reckoning make,
Than how to scramble at the shearers' feast,
And shove away the worthy bidden guest;
Blind mouths! that scarce themselves know how to hold
A sheep-hook, or have learned aught else the least   120
That to the faithful herdman's art belongs!
What recks it them?   What need they?   They are sped;
And when they list, their lean and flashy songs
Grate on their scrannel pipes of wretched straw;
The hungry sheep look up, and are not fed,   125
But, swoln with wind and the rank mist they draw,

Rot inwardly, and foul contagion spread:
Besides what the grim wolf with privy paw
Daily devours apace, and nothing said:
But that two-handed engine at the door   130
Stands ready to smite once, and smite no more."
    Return, Alpheus, the dread voice is past,
That shrunk thy streams; return, Sicilian Muse,
And call the values, and bid them hither cast
Their bells, and flowerets of a thousand hues.   135
Ye valleys low, where the mild whispers use
Of shades, and wanton winds, and gushing brooks,
On whose fresh lap the swart-star sparely looks;
Throw hither all your quaint enamelled eyes,
That on the green turf suck the honied showers,   140
And purple all the ground with vernal flowers.
Bring the rathe primrose that forsaken dies,
The tufted crowtoe, and pale jessamine,
The white pink, and the pansy freaked with jet,
The glowing violet,   145
The musk-rose, and the well-attired woodbine,
With cowslips wan that hang the pensive head,
And every flower that sad embroidery wears:
Bid amaranthus all his beauty shed,
And daffodillies fill their cups with tears,   150
To strew the laureate herse where Lycid lies.
For, so to interpose a little ease,
Let our frail thoughts dally with false surmise;
Ay me! Whilst thee the shores and sounding seas
Wash far away, where'er thy bones are hurled,   155
Whether beyond the stormy Hebrides,
Where thou perhaps, under the whelming tide,
Visit'st the bottom of the monstrous world;
Or whether thou, to our moist vows denied,
Sleep'st by the fable of Bellerus old,   160
Where the great vision of the guarded Mount
Looks towards Namancos and Bayona's hold;
Look homeward, angel, now, and melt with ruth:
And, O ye dolphins, waft the hapless youth.
    Weep no more, woeful Shepherds, weep no more,   165
For Lycidas your sorrow is not dead,
Sunk though he be beneath the watery floor;
So sinks the daystar in the ocean bed,
And yet anon repairs his drooping head,
And tricks his beams, and with new-spangled ore   170
Flames in the forehead of the morning sky:
So Lycidas sunk low, but mounted high,
Through the dear might of Him that walked the waves;
Where, other groves, and other streams along,

With nectar pure his oozy locks he laves, 175
And hears the unexpressive nuptial song,
In the blest kingdoms meek of joy and love.
There entertain him all the saints above,
In solemn troops, and sweet societies,
That sing, and, singing, in their glory move, 180
And wipe the tears for ever from his eyes.
Now, Lycidas, the shepherds weep no more;
Henceforth thou art the genius of the shore,
In thy large recompense, and shalt be good
To all that wander in that perilous flood. 185
   Thus sang the uncouth swain to the oaks and rills,
While the still morn went out with sandals gray;
He touched the tender stops of various quills,
With eager thought warbling his doric lay:
And now the sun had stretched out all the hills, 190
And now was dropt into the western bay:
At last he rose, and twitched his mantle blue:
Tomorrow to fresh woods, and pastures new.

On the Lord General Fairfax at the Siege of Colchester

Fairfax, whose name in arms through Europe rings,
   Filling each mouth with envy or with praise,
   And all her jealous monarchs with amaze
   And rumours loud, that daunt remotest kings;
Thy firm unshaken virtue ever brings 5
   Victory home, though new rebellions raise
   Their hydra heads, and the false north displays
   Her broken league to imp their serpent wings.
O yet a nobler task awaits thy hand,
   (For what can war but endless war still breed?) 10
   Till truth and right from violence be freed,
And public faith cleared from the shameful brand
   Of public fraud.   In vain doth Valour bleed,
   While Avarice and Rapine share the land.

To the Lord General Cromwell

Cromwell, our chief of men, who through a cloud
   Not of war only, but detractions rude,
   Guided by faith and matchless fortitude
   To peace and truth thy glorious way hast ploughed,
And on the neck of crowned Fortune proud 5

Hast reared God's trophies, and his work pursued,
   While Darwen stream, with blood of Scots imbrued,
   And Dunbar field resounds thy praises loud,
And Worcester's laureate wreath.   Yet much remains
   To conquer still; Peace hath her victories   10
   No less renowned than War: New foes arise
Threatening to bind our souls with secular chains:
   Help us to save free conscience from the paw
   Of hireling wolves, whose gospel is their maw.

To Sir Henry Vane the Younger

Vane, young in years, but in sage counsel old,
   Than whom a better senator ne'er held
   The helm of Rome, when gowns, not arms, repelled
   The fierce Epirot and the African bold;
Whether to settle peace, or to unfold   5
   The drift of hollow states hard to be spelled;
   Then to advise how war may, best upheld,
   Move by her two main nerves, iron and gold,
In all her equipage: besides to know
   Both spiritual power and civil, what each means,   10
   What severs each, thou hast learned, which few have done:
The bounds of either sword to thee we owe:
   Therefore on thy firm hand Religion leans
   In peace, and reckons thee her eldest son.

On the Late Massacre in Piedmont

Avenge, O Lord, thy slaughtered saints, whose bones
   Lie scattered on the Alpine mountains cold;
   Even them who kept thy truth so pure of old,
   When all our fathers worshipt stocks and stones,
Forget not: in thy book record their groans   5
   Who were thy sheep, and in their ancient fold
   Slain by the bloody Piedmontese that rolled
   Mother with infant down the rocks.   Their moans
The vales redoubled to the hills, and they
   To heaven.   Their martyred blood and ashes sow   10
   O'er all the Italian fields, where still doth sway
The triple tyrant; that from these may grow
   A hundredfold, who, having learned thy way,
   Early may fly the Babylonian woe.

On his Blindness

When I consider how my light is spent
   Ere half my days, in this dark world and wide,
   And that one talent which is death to hide,
   Lodged with me useless, though my soul more bent
To serve therewith my maker, and present   5
   My true account, lest He, returning, chide;
   "Doth God exact day-labour, light denied?"
   I fondly ask: But Patience, to prevent
That murmur, soon replies, "God doth not need
   Either man's work, or his own gifts; who best   10
   Bear his mild yoke, they serve Him best; his state
Is kingly; thousands at his bidding speed,
   And post o'er land and ocean without rest;
   They also serve who only stand and wait."

To Cyriack Skinner

Cyriack, whose grandsire, on the royal bench
   Of British Themis, with no mean applause
   Pronounced, and in his volumes taught, our laws,
   Which others at their bar so often wrench;
Today deep thoughts resolve with me to drench   5
   In mirth that, after, no repenting draws;
   Let Euclid rest, and Archimedes pause,
And what the Swede intends, and what the French.
To measure life learn thou betimes, and know
   Toward solid good what leads the nearest way;   10
   For other things mild Heaven a time ordains,
And disapproves that care, though wise in show,
   That with superfluous burden loads the day,
   And, when God sends a cheerful hour, refrains.

To the Same

Cyriack, this three years day these eyes, though clear,
   To outward view, of blemish or of spot,
   Bereft of light, their seeing have forgot;
   Nor to their idle orbs doth sight appear
Of sun, or moon, or star, throughout the year,   5
   Or man, or woman.   Yet I argue not
   Against Heaven's hand or will, nor bate a jot
Of heart or hope; but still bear up and steer
Right onward.   What supports me, dost thou ask?

The conscience, friend, to have lost them overplied   10
In liberty's defence, my noble task,
Of which all Europe rings from side to side.
This thought might lead me through the world's vain mask
Content though blind, had I no better guide.

On his Deceased Wife

Methought I saw my late espoused saint
Brought to me, like Alcestis, from the grave,
Whom Jove's great son to her glad husband gave,
Rescued from death by force, though pale and faint.
Mine, as whom washed from spot of childbed taint   5
Purification in the old Law did save,
And such, as yet once more I trust to have
Full sight of her in Heaven without restraint,
Came vested all in white, pure as her mind:
Her face was veiled; yet to my fancied sight   10
Love, sweetness, goodness, in her person shined
So clear, as in no face with more delight.
But O, as to embrace me she inclined,
I waked; she fled; and day brought back my night.

Andrew Marvell
(1621–1678)

The Garden

How vainly men themselves amaze
To win the palm, the oak, or bays,
And their uncessant labours see
Crowned from some single herb or tree,
Whose short and narrow verged shade   5
Does prudently their toils upbraid;
While all flowers and all trees do close
To weave the garlands of repose.

Fair quiet, have I found thee here,
And innocence, thy sister dear!   10
Mistaken long, I sought you then
In busy companies of men;
Your sacred plants, if here below,
Only among the plants will grow.
Society is all but rude,   15
To this delicious solitude.

No white nor red was ever seen
So amorous as this lovely green.
Fond lovers, cruel as their flame,
Cut in these trees their mistress' name;   20
Little, alas, they know or heed
How far these beauties hers exceed!
Fair trees! wheresoe'er your barks I wound,
No name shall but your own be found.

When we have run our passion's heat,   25
Love hither makes his best retreat.
The gods that mortal beauty chase,
Still in a tree did end their race:
Apollo hunted Daphne so,
Only that she might laurel grow;   30
And Pan did after Syrinx speed,
Not as a nymph, but for a reed.

What wondrous life is this I lead!
Ripe apples drop about my head;

The luscious clusters of the vine   35
Upon my mouth do crush their wine;
The nectarine and curious peach
Into my hands themselves do reach;
Stumbling on melons as I pass,
Ensnared with flowers, I fall on grass.   40

Meanwhile the mind from pleasure less
Withdraws into its happiness;
The mind, that ocean where each kind
Does straight its own resemblance find,
Yet it creates, transcending these,   45
Far other worlds and other seas,
Annihilating all that's made
To a green thought in a green shade.

Here at the fountain's sliding foot,
Or at some fruit tree's mossy root,   50
Casting the body's vest aside,
My soul into the boughs does glide;
There like a bird it sits and sings,
Then whets, then combs its silver wings;
And till prepared for longer flight,   55
Waves in its plumes the various light.

Such was that happy garden-state,
While man there walked without a mate;
After a place so pure and sweet,
What other help could yet be meet!   60
But 'twas beyond a mortal's share
To wander solitary there;
Two paradises 'twere, in one,
To live in paradise alone.

How well the skillful gard'ner drew   65
Of flowers and herbs this dial new,
Where, from above, the milder sun
Does through a fragrant zodiac run;
And as it works, the industrious bee
Computes its time as well as we.   70
How could such sweet and wholesome hours
Be reckoned but with herbs and flowers?

On a Drop of Dew

See how the orient dew,
Shed from the bosom of the morn
    Into the blowing roses,

Yet careless of its mansion new,
For the clear region where 'twas born   5
   Round in itself encloses,
   And in its little globe's extent
Frames as it can its native element;
How it the purple flower does slight,
   Scarce touching where it lies,   10
But gazing back upon the skies,
   Shines with a mournful light
     Like its own tear,
Because so long divided from the sphere.
   Restless it rolls and unsecure,   15
    Trembling lest it grow impure,
   Till the warm sun pity its pain,
And to the skies exhale it back again.
   So the soul, that drop, that ray
Of the clear fountain of eternal day,   20
Could it within the human flower be seen,
    Rememb'ring still its former height,
   Shuns the sweet leaves and blossoms green;
    And recollecting its own light,
Does, in its pure and circling thoughts, express   25
The greater heaven in an heaven less.
   In how coy a figure wound,
   Every way it turns away;
   So the world excluding round,
   Yet receiving in the day;   30
   Dark beneath but bright above,
   Here disdaining, there in love;
   How loose and easy hence to go,
   How girt and ready to ascend;
   Moving but on a point below,   35
   It all about does upwards bend.
Such did the manna's sacred dew distil,
White and entire, though congealed and chill;
Congealed on earth, but does, dissolving, run
Into the glories of th' almighty sun.   40

The Mower against Gardens

Luxurious man, to bring his vice in use,
   Did after him the world seduce,
And from the fields the flowers and plants allure,
   Where nature was most plain and pure.
He first enclosed within the garden's square   5
   A dead and standing pool of air;
And a more luscious earth for them did knead,

Which stupefied them while it fed.
The pink grew then as double as his mind;
  The nutriment did change the kind.   10
With strange perfumes he did the roses taint;
  And flowers themselves were taught to paint.
The tulip, white, did for complexion seek,
  And learned to interline its cheek;
Its onion root they then so high did hold   15
  That one was for a meadow sold.
Another world was searched, through oceans new,
  To find the marvel of Peru.
And yet these rarities might be allowed
  To man, that sov'reign thing and proud,   20
Had he not dealt between the bark and tree,
  Forbidden mixtures there to see.
No plant now knew the stock from which it came;
  He grafts upon the wild the tame,
That the uncertain and adult'rate fruit   25
  Might put the palate in dispute.
His green seraglio has its eunuchs too,
  Lest any tyrant him outdo;
And in the cherry he does nature vex,
  To procreate without a sex.   30
'Tis all enforced, the fountain and the grot,
  While the sweet fields do lie forgot,
Where willing nature does to all dispense
  A wild and fragrant innocence;
And fauns and fairies do the meadows till   35
  More by their presence than their skill.
Their statues, polished by some ancient hand,
  May to adorn the gardens stand;
But howsoe'er the figures do excel,
  The gods themselves with us do dwell.   40

The Coronet

When for the thorns with which I long, too long,
  With many a piercing wound
  My Saviour's head have crowned,
I seek with garlands to redress that wrong;
  Through every garden, every mead,   5
I gather flowers (my fruits are only flowers),
  Dismantling all the fragrant towers
That once adorned my shepherdess's head.
And now when I have summed up all my store,
  Thinking, so I myself deceive,   10
  So rich a chaplet thence to weave

As never yet the King of Glory wore,
   Alas, I find the serpent old
   That twining in his speckled breast
   About the flowers disguised does fold   15
   With wreaths of fame and interest.
Ah, foolish man, that wouldst debase with them
And mortal glory, heaven's diadem!
But thou who only couldst the serpent tame,
Either his slippery knots at once unite   20
And disentangle all his winding snare,
Or shatter too with him my curious frame
And let these wither so that he may die,
Though set with skill and chosen out with care,
That they, while thou on both their spoils dost tread,   25
May crown thy feet, that could not crown thy head.

A Dialogue between the Soul and Body

Soul

Oh, who shall from this dungeon raise
A soul enslaved so many ways?
With bolts of bones; that fettered stands
In feet, and manacled in hands;
Here blinded with an eye, and there   5
Deaf with the drumming of an ear;
A soul hung up, as 'twere, in chains
Of nerves and arteries and veins;
Tortured, besides each other part,
In a vain head and double heart.   10

Body

Oh, who shall me deliver whole
From bonds of this tyrannic soul?
Which, stretched upright, impales me so
That mine own precipice I go;
And warms and moves this needless frame,   15
A fever could but do the same.
And, wanting where its spite to try,
Has made me live to let me die.
A body that could never rest,
Since this ill spirit it possessed.   20

Soul

What magic could me thus confine
Within another's grief to pine?

Where whatsoever it complain,
I feel, that cannot feel, the pain.
And all my care itself employs,   25
That to preserve which me destroys.
Constrained not only to endure
Diseases, but, what's worse, the cure;
And ready oft the port to gain,
Am shipwrecked into health again.   30

Body

But physic yet could never reach
The maladies thou me dost teach:
Whom first the cramp of hope does tear,
And then the palsy shakes of fear;
The pestilence of love does heat,   35
Or hatred's hidden ulcer eat.
Joy's cheerful madness does perplex,
Or sorrow's other madness vex;
Which knowledge forces me to know,
And memory will not forgo.   40
What but a soul could have the wit
To build me up for sin so fit?
So architects do square and hew
Green trees that in the forest grew.

Bermudas

Where the remote Bermudas ride
In th' ocean's bosom unespied,
From a small boat that rowed along,
The list'ning winds received this song:
  What should we do but sing his praise   5
That led us through the wat'ry maze
Unto an isle so long unknown,
And yet far kinder than our own?
Where he the huge sea-monsters wracks,
That lift the deep upon their backs,   10
He lands us on a grassy stage,
Safe from the storms and prelates' rage.
He gave us this eternal spring
Which here enamels everything,
And sends the fowls to us in care,   15
On daily visits through the air.
He hangs in shades the orange bright,
Like golden lamps in a green night;
And does in the pomegranates close

Jewels more rich than Ormus shows.   20
He makes the figs our mouths to meet
And throws the melons at our feet,
But apples plants of such a price,
No tree could ever bear them twice.
With cedars, chosen by his hand,   25
From Lebanon, he stores the land,
And makes the hollow seas that roar
Proclaim the ambergris on shore.
He cast, of which we rather boast,
The Gospel's pearl upon our coast,   30
And in these rocks for us did frame
A temple, where to sound his name.
Oh, let our voice his praise exalt,
Till it arrive at heaven's vault;
Which thence, perhaps, rebounding, may   35
Echo beyond the Mexic Bay.
   Thus sung they in the English boat
An holy and a cheerful note,
And all the way, to guide their chime,
With falling oars they kept the time.   40

The Nymph complaining for the Death of her Fawn

The wanton troopers riding by
Have shot my fawn, and it will die.
Ungentle men! they cannot thrive
To kill thee. Thou ne'er didst alive
Them any harm, alas, nor could   5
Thy death yet do them any good.
I'm sure I never wished them ill,
Nor do I for all this, nor will;
But if my simple prayers may yet
Prevail with heaven to forget   10
Thy murder, I will join my tears
Rather than fail. But oh, my fears!
It cannot die so. Heaven's King
Keeps register of everything,
And nothing may we use in vain.   15
Ev'n beasts must be with justice slain,
Else men are made their deodands;
Though they should wash their guilty hands
In this warm life-blood, which doth part
From thine, and wound me to the heart,   20
Yet could they not be clean, their stain
Is dyed in such a purple grain.
There is not such another in

The world to offer for their sin.
   Unconstant Sylvio, when yet   25
I had not found him counterfeit,
One morning, I remember well,
Tied in this silver chain and bell,
Gave it to me; nay, and I know
What he said then, I'm sure I do.   30
Said he, Look how your huntsman here
Hath taught a fawn to hunt his *dear*.
But Sylvio soon had me beguiled.
This waxed tame, while he grew wild;
And quite regardless of my smart.   35
Left me his fawn, but took his heart.
   Thenceforth I set myself to play
My solitary time away,
With this, and very well content
Could so mine idle life have spent;   40
For it was full of sport, and light
Of foot and heart, and did invite
Me to its game; it seemed to bless
Itself in me. How could I less
Than love it? Oh, I cannot be   45
Unkind to a beast that loveth me.
   Had it lived long, I do not know
Whether it too might have done so
As Sylvio did; his gifts might be
Perhaps as false or more than he.   50
But I am sure, for aught that I
Could in so short a time espy,
Thy love was far more better then
The love of false and cruel men.
   With sweetest milk and sugar first   55
I it at mine own fingers nursed;
And as it grew, so every day
It waxed more white and sweet than they.
It had so sweet a breath! And oft
I blushed to see its foot more soft   60
And white, shall I say than my hand?
Nay, any lady's of the land.
   It is a wondrous thing how fleet
'Twas on those little silver feet;
With what a pretty skipping grace   65
It oft would challenge me the race;
And when 't had left me far away,
'Twould stay, and run again, and stay,
For it was nimbler much than hinds,
And trod as on the four winds.   70
   I have a garden of my own,

But so with roses overgrown
And lilies, that you would it guess
To be a little wilderness;
And all the spring time of the year 75
It only loved to be there.
Among the beds of lilies I
Have sought it oft, where it should lie;
Yet could not, till itself would rise,
Find it, although before mine eyes; 80
For in the flaxen lilies' shade,
It like a bank of lilies laid.
Upon the roses it would feed
Until its lips ev'n seemed to bleed,
And then to me 'twould boldly trip 85
And print those roses on my lip.
But all its chief delight was still
On roses thus itself to fill,
And its pure virgin limbs to fold
In whitest sheets of lilies cold. 90
Had it lived long it would have been
Lilies without, roses within.
   O help, O help! I see it faint
And die as calmly as a saint.
See how it weeps! The tears do come, 95
Sad, slowly dropping like a gum.
So weeps the wounded balsam, so
The holy frankincense doth flow;
The brotherless Heliades
Melt in such amber tears as these. 100
   I in a golden vial will
Keep these two crystal tears, and fill
It till it do o'erflow with mine,
Then place it in Diana's shrine.
   Now my sweet fawn is vanished to 105
Whither the swans and turtles go,
In fair Elysium to endure
With milk-white lambs and ermines pure.
O do not run too fast, for I
Will but bespeak thy grave, and die. 110
   First my unhappy statue shall
Be cut in marable, and withal
Let it be weeping too; but there
The engraver sure his art may spare,
For I so truly thee bemoan 115
That I shall weep though I be stone,
Until my tears, still dropping, wear
My breast, themselves engraving there.
There at my feet shalt thou be laid,

Of purest alabaster made;   120
For I would have thine image be
White as I can, though not as thee.

The Picture of Little T. C. in a Prospect of Flowers

See with what simplicity
This nymph begins her golden days!
In the green grass she loves to lie,
And there with her fair aspect tames
The wilder flowers, and gives them names;   5
But only with the roses plays,
    And them does tell
What color best becomes them, and what smell.

Who can foretell for what high cause
This darling of the gods was born?   10
Yet this is she whose chaster laws
The wanton Love shall one day fear,
And under her command severe
See his bow broke and ensigns torn.
    Happy, who can   15
Appease this virtuous enemy of man!

Oh, then let me in time compound,
And parley with those conquering eyes,
Ere they have tried their force to wound,
Ere with their glancing wheels they drive   20
In triumph over hearts that strive,
And them that yield but more despise.
    Let me be laid
Where I may see thy glories from some shade.

Meantime, whilst every verdant thing   25
Itself does at thy beauty charm,
Reform the errors of the spring:
Make that the tulips may have share
Of sweetness, seeing they are fair;
And roses of their thorns disarm;   30
    But most procure
That violets may a longer age endure.

But, O young beauty of the woods,
Whom nature courts with fruits and flowers,
Gather the flowers, but spare the buds,   35
Lest Flora, angry at thy crime,
To kill her infants in their prime,
Do quickly make the example yours;

And ere we see,
Nip in the blossom all our hopes and thee.   40

To his Coy Mistress

Had we but world enough, and time,
This coyness, lady, were no crime.
We would sit down and think which way
To walk, and pass our long love's day;
Thou by the Indian Ganges' side   5
Shouldst rubies find; I by the tide
Of Humber would complain. I would
Love you ten years before the Flood;
And you should, if you please, refuse
Till the conversion of the Jews.   10
My vegetable love should grow
Vaster than empires, and more slow.
An hundred years should go to praise
Thine eyes, and on thy forehead gaze;
Two hundred to adore each breast,   15
But thirty thousand to the rest;
An age at least to every part,
And the last age should show your heart.
For, lady, you deserve this state,
Nor would I love at lower rate.   20
    But at my back I always hear
Time's winged chariot hurrying near;
And yonder all before us lie
Deserts of vast eternity.
Thy beauty shall no more be found,   25
Nor in thy marble vault shall sound
My echoing song; then worms shall try
That long preserved virginity,
And your quaint honour turn to dust,
And into ashes all my lust.   30
The grave's a fine and private place,
But none, I think, do there embrace.
    Now therefore, while the youthful hue
Sits on thy skin like morning dew,
And while thy willing soul transpires   35
At every pore with instant fires,
Now let us sport us while we may;
And now, like amorous birds of prey,
Rather at once our time devour,
Than languish in his slow-chapped power.   40
Let us roll all our strength, and all
Our sweetness, up into one ball;

And tear our pleasures with rough strife
Thorough the iron gates of life.
Thus, though we cannot make our sun   45
Stand still, yet we will make him run.

An Horatian Ode upon Cromwell's Return from Ireland

The forward youth that would appear
Must now forsake his muses dear,
   Nor in the shadows sing
   His numbers languishing.
'Tis time to leave the books in dust,   5
And oil the unused armour's rust,
   Removing from the wall
   The corslet of the hall.
So restless Cromwell could not cease
In the inglorious arts of peace,   10
   But through advent'rous war
   Urged his active star.
And like the three-forked lightning, first
Breaking the clouds where it was nursed,
   Did through his own side   15
   His fiery way divide.
For 'tis all one to courage high,
The emulous or enemy;
   And with such to enclose
   Is more than to oppose.   20
Then burning through the air he went,
And palaces and temples rent;
   And Caesar's head at last
   Did through his laurels blast.
'Tis madness to resist or blame   25
The force of angry heaven's flame;
   And if we would speak true,
   Much to the man is due,
Who from his private gardens where
He lived reserved and austere,   30
   As if his highest plot
   To plant the bergamot,
Could by industrious valour climb
To ruin the great work of time,
   And cast the kingdom old   35
   Into another mold,
Though justice against fate complain,
And plead the ancient rights in vain;
   But those do hold or break

    As men are strong or weak.   40
Nature that hateth emptiness
Allows of penetration less,
    And therefore must make room
    Where greater spirits come.
What field of all the civil wars   45
Where his were not the deepest scars?
    And Hampton shows what part
    He had of wiser art,
Where, twining subtile fears with hope,
He wove a net of such a scope   50
    That Charles himself might chase
    To Carisbrooke's narrow case,
That thence the royal actor borne
The tragic scaffold might adorn,
    While round the armed bands   55
    Did clap their bloody hands.
He nothing common did or mean
Upon that memorable scene,
    But with his keener eye
    The axe's edge did try;   60
Nor called the gods with vulgar spite
To vindicate his helpless right,
    But bowed his comely head
    Down as upon a bed.
This was that memorable hour   65
Which first assured the forced power.
    So when they did design
    The Capitol's first line,
A bleeding head, where thy begun,
Did fright the architects to run;   70
    And yet in that the state
    Foresaw its happy fate.
And now the Irish are ashamed
To see themselves in one year tamed;
    So much one man can do   75
    That does both act and know.
They can affirm his praises best,
And have, though overcome, confessed
    How good he is, how just,
    And fit for highest trust;   80
Nor yet grown stiffer with command,
But still in the republic's hand;
    How fit he is to sway
    That can so well obey.
He to the Commons' feet presents   85
A kingdom for his first year's rents;
    And, what he may, forbears

His fame, to make it theirs,
And has his sword and spoils ungirt,
To lay them at the public's skirt.   90
    So when the falcon high
    Falls heavy from the sky,
She, having killed, no more does search
But on the next green bough to perch,
    Where, when he first does lure,   95
    The falconer has her sure.
What may not then our isle presume
While victory his crest does plume!
    What may not others fear
    If thus he crown each year!   100
A Caesar he ere long to Gaul,
To Italy an Hannibal,
    And to all states not free,
    Shall climacteric be.
The Pict no shelter now shall find   105
Within his parti-coloured mind;
    But from this valour sad
    Shrink underneath the plaid,
Happy if in the tufted brake
The English hunter him mistake,   110
    Nor lay his hounds in near
    The Caledonian deer.
But thou, the war's and fortune's son,
March indefatigably on;
    And for the last effect   115
    Still keep thy sword erect;
Besides the force it has to fright
The spirits of the shady night,
    The same arts that did gain
    A power, must it maintain.   120

Tom May's Death

As one put drunk into the packet-boat,
Tom May was hurried hence and did not know't.
But was amazed on the Elysian side,
And with an eye uncertain, gazing wide,
Could not determine in what place he was,   5
(For whence, in Stephen's Alley, trees or grass?)
Nor where The Pope's Head, nor The Mitre lay,
Signs by which still he found and lost his way.
At last while doubtfully he all compares,
He saw near hand, as he imagined, Ares.   10

Such did he seem for corpulence and port,
But 'twas a man much of another sort;
'Twas Ben that in the dusky laurel shade
Amongst the chorus of old poets layed,
Sounding of ancient heroes, such as were   15
The subjects' safety, and the rebels' fear,
And how a double-headed vulture eats
Brutus and Cassius, the people's cheats.
But seeing May, he varied straight his song,
Gently to signify that he was wrong.   20
'Cups more than civil of Emathian wine,
I sing' (said he) 'and the Pharsalian Sign,
Where the historian of the commonwealth
In his own bowels sheathed the conquering health.'
By this, May to himself and them was come,   25
He found he was translated, and by whom,
Yet then with foot as stumbling as his tongue
Pressed for his place among the learned throng.
But Ben, who knew not neither foe nor friend,
Sworn enemy to all that do pretend,   30
Rose; more than ever he was seen severe,
Shook his gray locks, and his own bays did tear
At this intrusion. Then with laurel wand—
The awful sign of his supreme command,
At whose dread whisk Virgil himself does quake,   35
And Horace patiently its stroke does take—
As he crowds in, he whipped him o'er the pate
Like Pembroke at the masque, and then did rate:
    'Far from these blessed shades tread back again
Most servile wit, and mercenary pen,   40
Polydore, Lucan, Alan, Vandal, Goth,
Malignant poet and historian both—
Go seek the novice statesmen, and obtrude
On them some Roman cast similitude,
Tell them of liberty, the stories fine,   45
Until you all grow consuls in your wine;
Or thou, dictator of the glass, bestow
On him the Cato, this the Cicero,
Transferring old Rome hither in your talk,
As Bethlem's House did to Loreto walk.   50
Foul architect, that hadst not eye to see
How ill the measures of these states agree,
And who by Rome's example England lay,
Those but to Lucan do continue May.
But thee nor ignorance nor seeming good   55
Misled, but malice fixed and understood.
Because some one than thee more worthy wears
The sacred laurel, hence are all these tears?

Must therefore all the world be set on flame,
Because a gazette-writer missed his aim?   60
And for a tankard-bearing muse must we
As for the basket, Guelphs and Ghibellines be?
When the sword glitters o'er the judge's head,
And fear has coward churchmen silenced,
Then is the poet's time, 'tis then he draws,   65
And single fights forsaken virtue's cause.
He, when the wheel of empire whirleth back,
And though the world's disjointed axle crack,
Sings still of ancient rights and better times,
Seeks wretched good, arraigns successful crimes.   70
But thou, base man, first prostituted hast
Our spotless knowledge and the studies chaste,
Apostatizing from our arts and us,
To turn the chronicler to Spartacus.
Yet wast thou taken hence with equal fate   75
Before thou couldst great Charles's death relate.
But what will deeper wound thy little mind,
Hast left surviving Davenant still behind,
Who laughs to see in this thy death renewed,
Right Roman poverty and gratitude.   80
Poor poet thou, and grateful senate they,
Who thy last reckoning did so largely pay,
And with the public gravity would come,
When thou hadst drunk thy last to lead thee home,
If that can be thy home where Spenser lies,   85
And reverend Chaucer, but their dust does rise
Against thee, and expels thee from their side,
As the eagle's plumes from other birds divide.
Nor here thy shade must dwell. Return, return,
Where sulphury Phlegethon does ever burn.   90
Thee Cerberus with all his jaws shall gnash,
Megaera thee with all her serpents lash.
Thou riveted unto Ixion's wheel
Shalt break, and the perpetual vulture feel.
'Tis just, what torments poets e'er did feign,   95
Thou first historically shouldst sustain.'
    Thus, by irrevocable sentence cast,
May, only Master of these Revels, passed.
And straight he vanished in a cloud of pitch,
Such as unto the Sabbath bears the witch.   100

Upon Appleton House

TO THE LORD FAIRFAX

1

Within this sober frame expect
Work of no foreign architect
That unto caves the quarries drew,
And forests did to pastures hew,
Who of his great design in pain   5
Did for a model vault his brain,
Whose columns should so high be raised
To arch the brows that on them gazed.

2

Why should of all things man unruled
Such unproportioned dwellings build?   10
The beasts are by their dens expressed:
And birds contrive an equal nest;
The low-roofed tortoises do dwell
In cases fit of tortoise shell:
No creature loves an empty space;   15
Their bodies measure out their place.

3

But he, superfluously spread,
Demands more room alive than dead;
And in his hollow palace goes
Where winds (as he) themselves may lose;   20
What need of all this marble crust
T'impark the wanton mote of dust,
That thinks by breadth the world t'unite
Though the first builders failed in height?

4

But all things are composed here   25
Like Nature, orderly and near:
In which we the dimensions find
Of that more sober age and mind,
When larger-sized men did stoop
To enter at a narrow loop;   30
As practising, in doors so strait,
To strain themselves through heaven's gate.

5

And surely when the after age
Shall hither come in pilgrimage,

These sacred places to adore,   35
By Vere and Fairfax trod before,
Men will dispute how their extent
Within such dwarfish confines went:
And some will smile at this, as well
As Romulus his bee-like cell.   40

6

Humility alone designs
Those short but admirable lines,
By which, ungirt and unconstrained,
Things greater are in less contained.
Let others vainly strive t'immure   45
The circle in the quadrature!
These holy mathematics can
In every figure equal man.

7

Yet thus the laden house does sweat,
And scarce endures the master great: 50
But where he comes the swelling hall
Stirs, and the square grows spherical,
More by his magnitude distressed,
Then he is by its straitness pressed:
And too officiously it slights   55
That in itself which him delights.

8

So honour better lowness bears,
Than that unwonted greatness wears:
Height with a certain grace does bend,
But low things clownishly ascend.   60
And yet what needs there here excuse,
Where everything does answer use?
Where neatness nothing can condemn,
Nor pride invent what to contemn?

9

A stately frontispiece of poor   65
Adorns without the open door:
Nor less the rooms within commends
Daily new furniture of friends.
The house was built upon the place
Only as for a mark of grace;   70
And for an inn to entertain
Its lord a while, but not remain.

10

Him Bishop's Hill or Denton may,
Or Bilbrough, better hold than they:
But Nature here hath been so free   75
As if she said, 'Leave this to me.'
Art would more neatly have defaced
What she had laid so sweetly waste,
In fragrant gardens, shady woods,
Deep meadows, and transparent floods.   80

11

While with slow eyes we these survey,
And on each pleasant footstep stay,
We opportunely may relate
The progress of this house's fate.
A nunnery first gave it birth   85
(For virgin buildings oft brought forth);
And all that neighbour-ruin shows
The quarries whence this dwelling rose.

12

Near to this gloomy cloister's gates
There dwelt the blooming virgin Thwaites,   90
Fair beyond measure, and an heir
Which might deformity make fair.
And oft she spent the summer suns
Discoursing with the subtle nuns.
Whence in these words one to her weaved,   95
(As 'twere by chance) thoughts long conceived.

13

'Within this holy leisure we
Live innocently, as you see.
These walls restrain the world without,
But hedge our liberty about.   100
These bars enclose that wider den
Of those wild creatures called men.
The cloister outward shuts its gates,
And, from us, locks on them the grates.

14

'Here we, in shining armour white,   105
Like virgin amazons do fight.
And our chaste lamps we hourly trim,
Lest the great Bridegroom find them dim.
Our orient breaths perfumed are

With incense of incessant prayer.   110
And holy-water of our tears
Most strangely our complexion clears.

15

'Not tears of grief; but such as those
With which calm pleasure overflows;
Or pity, when we look on you   115
That live without this happy vow.
How should we grieve that must be seen
Each one a spouse, and each a queen,
And can in heaven hence behold
Our brighter robes and crowns of gold?   120

16

'When we have prayed all our beads,
Someone the holy legend reads;
While all the rest with needles paint
The face and graces of the saint.
But what the linen can't receive   125
They in their lives do interweave.
This work the saints best represents;
That serves for altar's ornaments.

17

'But much it to our work would add
If here your hand, your face we had: 130
By it we would Our Lady touch;
Yet thus she you resembles much.
Some of your features, as we sewed,
Through every shrine should be bestowed.
And one in beauty we would take   135
Enough a thousand saints to make.

18

'And (for I dare not quench the fire
That me does for your good inspire)
'Twere sacrilege a man t'admit
To holy things, for heaven fit.   140
I see the angels in a crown
On you the lilies showering down:
And around about you glory breaks,
That something more than human speaks.

19

'All beauty, when at such a height,   145
Is so already consecrate.
Fairfax I know; and long ere this

Have marked the youth, and what he is.
But can he such a rival seem
For whom you heaven should disesteem?   150
Ah, no! and 'twould more honour prove
He your *devoto* were, than love.

20
'Here live beloved, and obeyed:
Each one your sister, each your maid.
And, if our rule seem strictly penned,   155
The rule itself to you shall bend.
Our abbess too, now far in age,
Doth your succession near presage.
How soft the yoke on us would lie
Might such fair hands as yours it tie!   160

21
'Your voice, the sweetest of the choir,
Shall draw heaven nearer, raise us higher.
And your example, if our head,
Will soon us to perfection lead.
Those virtues to us all so dear,   165
Will straight grow sanctity when here:
And that, once sprung, increase so fast
Till miracles it work at last.

22
'Nor is our order yet so nice,
Delight to banish as a vice.   170
Here pleasure piety doth meet;
One perfecting the other sweet.
So through the mortal fruit we boil
The sugar's uncorrupting oil:
And that which perished while we pull,   175
Is thus preserved clear and full.

23
'For such indeed are all our arts,
Still handling Nature's finest parts.
Flowers dress the altars; for the clothes,
The sea-born amber we compose;   180
Balms for the grieved we draw; and pastes
We mould, as baits for curious tastes.
What need is here of man? unless
These as sweet sins we should confess.

24
'Each night among us to your side   185
Appoint a fresh and virgin bride;

Whom if our Lord at midnight find,
Yet neither should be left behind.
Where you may lie as chaste in bed,
As pearls together billeted,   190
All night embracing arm in arm
Like crystal pure with cotton warm.

25
'But what is this to all the store
Of joys you see, and may make more!
Try but a while, if you be wise: 195
The trial neither costs, nor ties.'
Now, Fairfax, seek her promised faith:
Religion that dispensed hath,
Which she henceforward does begin;
The nun's smooth tongue has sucked her in.   200

26
Oft, though he knew it was in vain,
Yet would he valiantly complain.
'Is this that sanctity so great,
An art by which you finelier cheat?
Hypocrite witches, hence avaunt,   205
Who though in prison yet enchant!
Death only can such thieves make fast,
As rob though in the dungeon cast.

27
'Were there but, when this house was made,
One stone that a just hand had laid,   210
It must have fall'n upon her head
Who first thee from thy faith misled.
And yet, how well soever meant,
With them 'twould soon grow fraudulent;
For like themselves they alter all,   215
And vice infects the very wall.

28
'But sure those buildings last not long,
Founded by folly, kept by wrong.
I know what fruit their gardens yield,
When they it think by night concealed.   220
Fly from their vices. 'Tis thy state,
Not thee, that they would consecrate.
Fly from their ruin. How I fear,
Though guiltless, lest thou perish there.'

29
What should he do? He would respect   225
Religion, but not right neglect:

For first religion taught him right,
And dazzled not but cleared his sight.
Sometimes resolved, his sword he draws,
But reverenceth then the laws: 230
For justice still that courage led;
First from a judge, then soldier bred.

30

Small honour would be in the storm.
The court him grants the lawful form;
Which licensed either peace or force, 235
To hinder the unjust divorce.
Yet still the nuns his right debarred,
Standing upon their holy guard.
Ill-counselled women, do you know
Whom you resist, or what you do? 240

31

Is not this he whose offspring fierce
Shall fight through all the universe;
And with successive valour try
France, Poland, either Germany;
Till one, as long since prophesied, 245
His horse through conquered Britain ride?
Yet, against fate, his spouse they kept,
And the great race would intercept.

32

Some to the breach against their foes
Their wooden saints in vain oppose. 250
Another bolder stands at push
With their old holy-water brush.
While the disjointed abbess threads
The jingling chain-shot of her beads.
But their loudest cannon were their lungs; 255
And sharpest weapons were their tongues.

33

But waving these aside like flies,
Young Fairfax through the wall does rise.
Then th' unfrequented vault appeared,
And superstitions vainly feared. 260
The relics false were set to view;
Only the jewels there were true—
But truly bright and holy Thwaites
That weeping at the altar waits.

34

But the glad youth away her bears, 265
And to the nuns bequeaths her tears;

Who guiltily their prize bemoan,
Like gypsies that a child had stolen.
Thenceforth (as when the enchantment ends,
The castle vanishes or rends)   270
The wasting cloister with the rest
Was in one instant dispossessed.

35

At the demolishing, this seat
To Fairfax fell as by escheat.
And what both nuns and founders willed   275
'Tis likely better thus fulfilled.
For if the virgin proved not theirs,
The cloister yet remained hers.
Though many a nun there made her vow,
'Twas no religious house till now.   280

36

From that blest bed the hero came,
Whom France and Poland yet does fame:
Who, when retired here to peace,
His warlike studies could not cease;
But laid these gardens out in sport   285
In the just figure of a fort;
And with five bastions it did fence,
As aiming one for every sense.

37

When in the east the morning ray
Hangs out the colours of the day,   290
The bee through these known alleys hums,
Beating the *dian* with its drums.
Then flowers their drowsy eyelids raise,
Their silken ensigns each displays,
And dries its pan yet dank with dew,   295
And fills its flask with odours new.

38

These, as their governor goes by,
In fragrant volleys they let fly;
And to salute their governess
Again as great a charge they press: 300
None for the virgin nymph; for she
Seems with the flowers a flower to be.
And think so still! though not compare
With breath so sweet, or cheek so fair.

39

Well shot, ye firemen! Oh how sweet,   305
And round your equal fires do meet,

Whose shrill report no ear can tell,
But echoes to the eye and smell.
See how the flowers, as at parade,
Under their colours stand displayed: 310
Each regiment in order grows,
That of the tulip, pink, and rose.

40
But when the vigilant patrol
Of stars walks round about the Pole,
Their leaves, that to the stalks are curled,   315
Seem to their staves the ensigns furled.
Then in some flower's beloved hut
Each bee as sentinel is shut,
And sleeps so too: but, if once stirred,
She runs you through, or asks the word.   320

41
Oh thou, that dear and happy isle
The garden of the world erewhile,
Thou paradise of four seas,
Which heaven planted us to please,
But, to exclude the world, did guard   325
With watery if not flaming sword;
What luckless apple did we taste,
To make us mortal, and thee waste?

42
Unhappy! shall we never more
That sweet militia restore,   330
When gardens only had their towers,
And all the garrisons were flowers,
When roses only arms might bear,
And men did rosy garlands wear?
Tulips, in several colours barred,   335
Were then the Switzers of our Guard.

43
The gardener had the soldier's place,
And his more gentle forts did trace.
The nursery of all things green
Was then the only magazine.   340
The winter quarters were the stoves,
Where he the tender plants removes.
But war all this doth overgrow;
We ordnance plant and powder sow.

44

And yet their walks one on the sod   345
Who, had it pleased him and God,
Might once have made our gardens spring
Fresh as his own and flourishing.
But he preferred to the Cinque Ports
These five imaginary forts,   350
And, in those half-dry trenches, spanned
Power which the ocean might command.

45

For he did, with his utmost skill,
Ambition weed, but conscience till—
Conscience, that heaven-nursed plant,   355
Which most our earthly gardens want.
A prickling leaf it bears, and such
As that which shrinks at every touch;
But flowers eternal, and divine,
That in the crowns of saints do shine.   360

46

The sight does from these bastions ply,
The invisible artillery;
And at proud Cawood Castle seems
To point the battery of its beams.
As if it quarrelled in the seat   365
The ambition of its prelate great.
But o'er the meads below it plays,
Or innocently seems to gaze.

47

And now to the abyss I pass
Of that unfathomable grass,   370
Where men like grasshoppers appear—
But grasshoppers are giants there:
They, in their squeaking laugh, contemn
Us as we walk more low than them:
And, from the precipices tall   375
Of the green spires, to us do call.

48

To see men through this meadow dive,
We wonder how they rise alive,
As, under water, none does know
Whether he fall through it or go.   380
But, as the mariners that sound,

And show upon their lead the ground,
They bring up flowers so to be seen,
And prove they've at the bottom been.

49

No scene that turns with engines strange   385
Does oftener than these meadows change.
For when the sun the grass hath vexed,
The tawny mowers enter next;
Who seem like Israelites to be,
Walking on foot through a green sea.   390
To them the grassy deeps divide,
And crowd a lane to either side.

50

With whistling scythe, and elbow strong,
These massacre the grass along:
While one, unknowing, carves the rail,   395
Whose yet unfeathered quills her fail.
The edge all bloody from its breast
He draws, and does his stroke detest,
Fearing the flesh untimely mowed
To him a fate as black forebode.   400

51

But bloody Thestylis, that waits
To bring the mowing camp their cates,
Greedy as kites, has trussed it up,
And forthwith means on it to sup:
When on another quick she lights,   405
And cries, 'He called us Israelites;
But now, to make his saying true,
Rails rain for quails, for manna, dew.'

52

Unhappy birds! what does it boot
To build below the grass's root;
When lowness is unsafe as height,   410
And chance o'ertakes, what 'scapeth spite?
And now your orphan parents' call
Sounds your untimely funeral.
Death-trumpets creak in such a note,
And 'tis the sourdine in their throat.   415

53

Or sooner hatch or higher build:
The mower now commands the field,

In whose new traverse seemeth wrought
A camp of battle newly fought: 420
Where, as the meads with hay, the plain
Lies quilted o'er with bodies slain:
The women that with forks it fling
Do represent the pillaging.

54
And now the careless victors play,   425
Dancing the triumphs of the hay;
Where every mower's wholesome heat
Smells like an Alexander's sweat.
Their females fragrant as the mead
Which they in fairy circles tread: 430
When at their dance's end they kiss,
Their new-made hay not sweeter is.

55
When after this 'tis piled in cocks,
Like a calm sea it shows the rocks,
We wondering in the river near   435
How boats among them safely steer;
Or, like the desert Memphis sand,
Short pyramids of hay do stand.
And such the Roman camps do rise
In hills for soldiers' obsequies.   440

56
This scene again withdrawing brings
A new and empty face of things,
A levelled space, as smooth and plain
As cloths for Lely stretched to stain.
The world when first created sure   445
Was such a table rase and pure.
Or rather such is the *toril*
Ere the bulls enter at Madril.

57
For to this naked equal flat,
Which Levellers take pattern at,   450
The villagers in common chase
Their cattle, which it closer rase;
And what below the scythe increased
Is pinched yet nearer by the beast.
Such, in the painted world, appeared   455
Davenant with the universal herd.

58

They seem within the polished grass
A landskip drawn in looking-glass,
And shrunk in the huge pasture show
As spots, so shaped, on faces do—   460
Such fleas, ere they approach the eye,
In multiplying glasses lie.
They feed so wide, so slowly move,
As constellations do above.

59

Then, to conclude these pleasant acts,   465
Denton sets ope its cataracts,
And makes the meadow truly be
(What it but seemed before) a sea.
For, jealous of its lord's long stay,
It tries t'invite him thus away.   470
The river in itself is drowned,
And isles the astonished cattle round.

60

Let others tell the paradox,
How eels now bellow in the ox;
How horses at their tails do kick,   475
Turned as they hang to leeches quick;
How boats can over bridges sail;
And fishes do the stables scale.
How salmons trespassing are found;
And pikes are taken in the pound.   480

61

But I, retiring from the flood,
Take sanctuary in the wood,
And, while it lasts, myself embark
In this yet green, yet growing ark,
Where the first carpenter might best   485
Fit timber for his keel have pressed.
And where all creatures might have shares,
Although in armies, not in pairs.

62

The double wood of ancient stocks,
Linked in so thick, a union locks,   490
It like two pedigrees appears,
On th' one hand Fairfax, th' other Vere's:
Of whom though many fell in war,

Yet more to heaven shooting are:
And, as they Nature's cradle decked,   495
Will in green age her hearse expect.

63
When first the eye this forest sees
It seems indeed as wood not trees:
As if their neighbourhood so old
To one great trunk them all did mould.   500
There the huge bulk takes place, as meant
To thrust up a fifth element,
And stretches still so closely wedged
As if the night within were hedged.

64
Dark all without it knits; within   505
It opens passable and thin;
And in as loose an order grows
As the Corinthian porticoes.
The arching boughs unite between
The columns of the temple green;   510
And underneath the winged choirs
Echo about their tuned fires.

65
The nightingale does here make choice
To sing the trials of her voice.
Low shrubs she sits in, and adorns   515
With music high the squatted thorns.
But highest oaks stoop down to hear,
And listening elders prick the ear.
The thorn, lest it should hurt her, draws
Within the skin its shrunken claws.   520

66
But I have for my music found
A sadder, yet more pleasing sound:
The stockdoves, whose fair necks are graced
With nuptial rings, their ensigns chaste;
Yet always, for some cause unknown,   525
Sad pair unto the elms they moan.
O why should such a couple mourn,
That in so equal flames do burn!

67
Then as I careless on the bed
Of gelid strawberries do tread,   530
And through the hazels thick espy

The hatching throstle's shining eye,
The heron from the ash's top
The eldest of its young lets drop,
As if it stork-like did pretend 535
That tribute to its lord to send.

68

But most the hewel's wonders are,
Who here has the holtfelster's care.
He walks still upright from the root,
Measuring the timber with his foot, 540
And all the way, to keep it clean,
Doth from the bark the woodmoths glean.
He, with his beak, examines well
Which fit to stand and which to fell.

69

The good he numbers up, and hacks, 545
As if he marked them with the axe,
But where he, tinkling with his beak,
Does find the hollow oak to speak,
That for his building he designs,
And through the tainted side he mines. 550
Who could have thought the tallest oak
Should fall by such a feeble stroke!

70

Nor would it, had the tree not fed
A traitor-worm, within it bred,
(As first our flesh corrupt within 555
Tempts impotent and bashful sin).
And yet that worm triumphs not long,
But serves to feed the hewel's young,
While the oak seems to fall content,
Viewing the treason's punishment. 560

71

Thus I, easy philosopher,
Among the birds and trees confer.
And little now to make me wants
Or of the fowls, or of the plants:
Give me but wings as they, and I 565
Straight floating on the air shall fly:
Or turn me but, and you shall see
I was but an inverted tree.

72

Already I begin to call
In their most learned original: 570

And where I language want, my signs
The bird upon the bough divines;
And more attentive there doth sit
Than if she were with lime-twigs knit.
No leaf does tremble in the wind   575
Which I, returning, cannot find.

73
Out of these scattered sibyl's leaves
Strange prophecies my fancy weaves:
And in one history consumes,
Like Mexique paintings, all the plumes.   580
What Rome, Greece, Palestine, ere said
I in this light mosaic read.
Thrice happy he who, not mistook,
Hath read in Nature's mystic book.

74
And see how chance's better wit   585
Could with a mask my studies hit!
The oak leaves me embroider all,
Between which caterpillars crawl:
And ivy, with familiar trails,
Me licks, and clasps, and curls, and hales.   590
Under this antic cope I move
Like some great prelate of the grove.

75
Then, languishing with ease, I toss
On pallets swoll'n of velvet moss,
While the wind, cooling through the boughs,   595
Flatters with air my panting brows.
Thanks for my rest, ye mossy banks;
And unto you, cool zephyrs, thanks,
Who, as my hair, my thoughts too shed,
And winnow from the chaff my head.   600

76
How safe, methinks, and strong, behind
These trees have I encamped my mind:
Where beauty, aiming at the heart,
Bends in some tree its useless dart;
And where the world no certain shot   605
Can make, or me it toucheth not.
But I on it securely play,
And gall its horsemen all the day.

77

Bind me, ye woodbines, in your twines,
Curl me about, ye gadding vines,   610
And, oh, so close your circles lace,
That I may never leave this place:
But lest your fetters prove too weak,
Ere I your silken bondage break,
Do you, O brambles, chain me too,   615
And, courteous briars, nail me through.

78

Here in the morning tie my chain,
Where the two woods have made a lane,
While, like a guard on either side,
The trees before their lord divide;   620
This, like a long and equal thread,
Betwixt two labyrinths does lead.
But where the floods did lately drown,
There at the evening stake me down.

79

For now the waves are fall'n and dried,   625
And now the meadows fresher dyed,
Whose grass, with moister colour dashed,
Seems as green silks but newly washed.
No serpent new nor crocodile
Remains behind our little Nile,   630
Unless itself you will mistake,
Among these meads the only snake.

80

See in what wanton harmless folds
It everywhere the meadow holds;
And its yet muddy back doth lick,   635
Till as a crystal mirror slick,
Where all things gaze themselves, and doubt
If they be in it or without.
And for his shade which therein shines,
Narcissus-like, the sun too pines.   640

81

Oh what a pleasure 'tis to hedge
My temples here with heavy sedge,
Abandoning my lazy side,
Stretched as a bank unto the tide,
Or to suspend my sliding foot   645

On th' osier's undermined root,
And in its branches tough to hang,
While at my lines the fishes twang!

82

But now away my hooks, my quills,
And angles—idle utensils.   650
The young Maria walks tonight:
Hide, trifling youth, thy pleasures slight.
'Twere shame that such judicious eyes
Should with such toys a man surprise;
She, that already is the law   655
Of all her sex, her age's awe.

83

See how loose Nature, in respect
To her, itself doth recollect;
And everything so whisht and fine,
Starts forthwith to its *bonne mine*.   660
The sun himself, of her aware,
Seems to descend with greater care;
And lest she see him go to bed,
In blushing clouds conceals his head.

84

So when the shadows laid asleep   665
From underneath these banks do creep,
And on the river as it flows
With eben shuts begin to close;
The modest halcyon comes in sight,
Flying betwixt the day and night;   670
And such a horror calm and dumb,
Admiring Nature does benumb.

85

The viscous air, wheres'e'er she fly,
Follows and sucks her azure dye;
The jellying stream compacts below,   675
If it might fix her shadow so;
The stupid fishes hang, as plain
As flies in crystal overta'en;
And men the silent scene assist,
Charmed with the sapphire-winged mist.   680

86

Maria such, and so doth hush
The world, and through the evening rush.
No new-born comet such a train

Draws through the sky, nor star new-slain.
For straight those giddy rockets fail,   685
Which from the putrid earth exhale,
But by her flames, in heaven tried,
Nature is wholly vitrified.

87
'Tis she that to these gardens gave
That wondrous beauty which they have;   690
She straightness on the woods bestows;
To her the meadow sweetness owes;
Nothing could make the river be
So crystal pure but only she;
She yet more pure, sweet, straight, and fair,   695
Than gardens, woods, meads, rivers are.

88
Therefore what first she on them spent,
They gratefully again present:
The meadow, carpets where to tread;
The garden, flow'rs to crown her head;   700
And for a glass, the limpid brook,
Where she may all her beauties look;
But, since she would not have them seen,
The wood about her draws a screen.

89
For she, to higher beauties raised,   705
Disdains to be for lesser praised.
She counts her beauty to converse
In all the languages as hers;
Nor yet in those herself employs
But for the wisdom, not the noise;   710
Nor yet that wisdom would affect,
But as 'tis heaven's dialect.

90
Blest nymph! that couldst so soon prevent
Those trains by youth against thee meant:
Tears (watery shot that pierce the mind);   715
And signs (love's cannon charged with wind);
True praise (that breaks through all defence);
And feigned complying innocence;
But knowing where this ambush lay,
She 'scaped the safe, but roughest way.   720

91
This 'tis to have been from the first
In a domestic heaven nursed,

Under the discipline severe
Of Fairfax, and the starry Vere;
Where not one object can come nigh   725
But pure and spotless as the eye;
And goodness doth itself entail
On females, if there want a male.

92

Go now, fond sex, that on your face
Do all your useless study place,   730
Nor once at vice your brows dare knit
Lest the smooth forehead wrinkled sit:
Yet your own face shall at you grin,
Thorough the black-bag of your skin,
When knowledge only could have filled   735
And virtue all those furrows tilled.

93

Hence she with graces more divine
Supplies beyond her sex the line;
And like a sprig of mistletoe
On the Fairfacian oak does grow;   740
Whence, for some universal good,
The priest shall cut the sacred bud,
While her glad parents most rejoice,
And make their destiny their choice.

94

Meantime, ye fields, springs, bushes, flowers,   745
Where yet she leads her studious hours,
(Till fate her worthily translates,
And find a Fairfax for our Thwaites),
Employ the means you have by her,
And in your kind yourselves prefer;   750
That, as all virgins she precedes,
So you all woods, streams, gardens, meads.

95

For you, Thessalian Tempe's seat
Shall now be scorned as obsolete;
Aranjuez, as less, disdained;   755
The Bel-Retiro as constrained;
But name not the Idalian grove—
For 'twas the seat of wanton love—
Much less the dead's Elysian Fields,
Yet nor to them your beauty yields.   760

96

'Tis not, what once it was, the world,
But a rude heap together hurled,
All negligently overthrown,
Gulfs, deserts, precipices, stone.
Your lesser world contains the same,   765
But in more decent order tame;
You, heaven's centre, Nature's lap,
And paradise's only map.

97

But now the salmon-fishers moist
Their leathern boats begin to hoist,   770
And like Antipodes in shoes,
Have shod their heads in their canoes.
How tortoise-like, but not so slow,
These rational amphibii go!
Let's in: for the dark hemisphere   775
Does now like one of them appear.

Henry Vaughan
(1621–1695)

The Seed growing Secretly

St Mark 4.26

If this world's friends might see but once
What some poor man may often feel,
Glory and gold and crowns and thrones
They would soon quit, and learn to kneel.

My dew, my dew, my early love,   5
My soul's bright food, thy absence kills!
Hover not long, eternal dove!
Life without thee is loose, and spills.

Something I had which long ago
Did learn to suck, and sip, and taste,   10
But now grown sickly, sad, and slow,
Doth fret and wrangle, pine and waste.

O spread thy sacred wings and shake
One living drop! one drop life keeps!
If pious griefs heaven's joys awake,   15
O fill his bottle, thy child weeps!

Slowly and sadly doth he grow,
And soon as left, shrinks back to ill;
O feed that life which makes him blow
And spread and open to thy will!   20

For thy eternal living wells
None stained or withered shall come near;
A fresh immortal green there dwells,
And spotless white is all the wear.

Dear, secret greenness! nursed below   25
Tempests and winds and winter nights,
Vex not that but one sees thee grow;
That One made all these lesser lights.

If those bright joys he singly sheds
On thee were all met in one crown,   30
Both sun and stars would hide their heads,
And moons, though full, would get them down.

Let glory be their bait, whose minds
Are all too high for a low cell;
Though hawks can prey through storms and winds,   35
The poor bee in her hive must dwell.

Glory, the crowd's cheap tinsel still
To what most takes them, is a drudge,
And they too oft take good for ill,
And thriving vice for virtue judge.   40

What needs a conscience calm and bright
Within itself an outward test?
Who breaks his glass to take more light,
Makes way for storms into his rest.

Then bless thy secret growth, nor catch   45
At noise, but thrive unseen and dumb;
Keep clean, bear fruit, earn life, and watch
Till the white-winged reapers come!

The Night

John 3.2

Through that pure virgin-shrine,
That sacred veil drawn o'er thy glorious noon,
That men might look and live, as glow-worms shine,
    And face the moon,
  Wise Nicodemus saw such light   5
  As made him know his God by night.

  Most blest believer he!
Who in that land of darkness and blind eyes
Thy long-expected healing wings could see
    When thou didst rise,   10
  And what can never more be done,
  Did at midnight speak with the Sun!

  Oh, who will tell me where
He found thee at that dead and silent hour!
What hallowed solitary ground did bear   15
    So rare a flower,
  Within whose sacred leaves did lie
  The fullness of the deity.

No mercy-seat of gold,
No dead and dusty cherub, nor carved stone,   20
But his own living works did my Lord hold
    And lodge alone,
    Where trees and herbs did watch and peep
    And wonder, while the Jews did sleep.

    Dear night! this world's defeat;   25
The stop to busy fools; care's check and curb;
The day of spirits; my soul's calm retreat
    Which none disturb;
    Christ's progress, and his prayer time;
    The hours to which high heaven doth chime;   30

    God's silent, searching flight;
When my Lord's head is filled with dew, and all
His locks are wet with the clear drops of night;
    His still, soft call;
    His knocking time; the soul's dumb watch,   35
    When spirits their fair kindred catch.

    Were all my loud, evil days
Calm and unhaunted as is thy dark tent,
Whose peace but by some angel's wing or voice
    Is seldom rent,   40
    Then I in heaven all the long year
    Would keep, and never wander here.

    But living where the sun
Doth all things wake, and where all mix and tire
Themselves and others, I consent and run   45
    To ev'ry mire,
    And by this world's ill-guiding light,
    Err more than I can do by night.

    There is in God, some say,
A deep but dazzling darkness, as men here   50
Say it is late and dusky, because they
    See not all clear;
    Oh, for that night, where I in him
    Might live invisible and dim!

The Morning Watch

O joys! infinite sweetness! with what flowers
And shoots of glory my soul breaks and buds!
    All the long hours
    Of night and rest,

　　　Through the still shrouds　　　　　　　　　5
　　　　Of sleep and clouds,
　　This dew fell on my breast;
　　　　Oh, how it bloods
And spirits all my earth! Hark! in what rings
And hymning circulations the quick world　　　10
　　　　Awakes and sings;
　　　　The rising winds
　　　　And falling springs,
　　　　Birds, beasts, all things
　　Adore him in their kinds.　　　　　　　　15
　　　　Thus all is hurled
In sacred hymns and order, the great chime
And symphony of nature. Prayer is
　　　　The world in tune,
　　　　A spirit voice,　　　　　　　　　　　20
　　　　And vocal joys
　　Whose echo is heav'n's bliss.
　　　　O let me climb
When I lie down! The pious soul by night
Is like a clouded star whose beams, though said　25
　　　　To shed their light
　　　　Under some cloud,
　　　　Yet are above,
　　　　And shine and move
　　Beyond that misty shroud.　　　　　　　30
　　　　So in my bed,
That curtained grave, though sleep like ashes hide
My lamp and life, both shall in thee abide.

Regeneration

1

A ward, and still in bonds, one day
　　　　I stole abroad,
It was high-spring, and all the way
　　　Primrosed and hung with shade;
　　　　Yet was it frost within,　　　　　　　5
　　　　　And surly winds
Blasted my infant buds, and sin
　　　Like clouds eclipsed my mind.

2

Stormed thus, I straight perceived my spring
　　　　　Mere stage and show,　　　　　10
My walk a monstrous, mountained thing
　　　Rough-cast with rocks and snow;

And as a pilgrim's eye
Far from relief,
Measures the melancholy sky   15
Then drops, and rains for grief,

3

So sighed I upwards still; at last
'Twixt steps, and falls
I reached the pinnacle, where placed
I found a pair of scales,   20
I took them up and laid
In the one late pains,
The other smoke, and pleasures weighed
But proved the heavier grains;

4

With that, some cried, "Away"; straight I   25
Obeyed, and led
Full east, a fair, fresh field could spy –
Some called it, Jacob's Bed;
A virgin-soil, which no
Rude feet e'er trod,   30
Where (since he stepped there) only go
Prophets, and friends of God.

5

Here, I reposed; but scarce well set,
A grove described
Of stately height, whose branches met   35
And mixed on every side;
I entered, and once in
(Amazed to see it)
Found all was changed, and a new spring
Did all my senses greet;   40

6

The unthrift sun shot vital gold
A thousand pieces,
And heaven its azure did unfold
Chequered with snowy fleeces,
The air was all in spice   45
And every bush
A garland wore; thus fed my eyes
But all the ear lay hush.

7

Only a little fountain lent
Some use for ears,   50
And on the dumb shades' language spent

The music of her tears;
I drew her near, and found
The cistern full
Of diverse stones, some bright, and round   55
Others ill-shaped, and dull.

8

The first (pray mark) as quick as light
Danced through the flood,
But, the last more heavy than the night
Nailed to the centre stood;   60
I wondered much, but tired
At last with thought,
My restless eye that still desired
As strange an object brought;

9

It was a bank of flowers, where I descried   65
(Though 'twas midday,)
Some fast asleep, others broad-eyed
And taking in the ray,
Here musing long, I heard
A rushing wind   70
Which still increased, but whence it stirred
Nor where I could not find;

10

I turned me round, and to each shade
Dispatched an eye,
To see, if any leaf had made   75
Least motion, or reply,
But while I listening sought
My mind to ease
By knowing, where 'twas, or where not,
It whispered; "Where I please."   80

"Lord", then said I, "On me one breath,
And let me die before my death!"

Arise O North, and come thou south-wind, and blow upon my garden, that the
spices thereof may flow out. Song of Solomon 4.16.

The Retreat

Happy those early days! when I
Shined in my angel-infancy.
Before I understood this place

Appointed for my second race,
Or taught my soul to fancy aught   5
But a white, celestial thought,
When yet I had not walked above
A mile or two from my first love,
And looking back (at that short space)
Could see a glimpse of his bright-face;   10
When on some gilded cloud or flower
My gazing soul would dwell an hour,
And in those weaker glories spy
Some shadows of eternity;
Before I taught my tongue to wound   15
My conscience with a sinful sound,
Or had the black art to dispense
A several sin to every sense,
But felt through all this fleshly dress
Bright shoots of everlastingness.   20
    O how I long to travel back
And tread again that ancient track!
That I might once more reach that plain,
Where first I left my glorious train,
From whence the enlightened spirit sees   25
That shady city of palm trees;
But ah! my soul with too much stay
Is drunk, and staggers in the way.
Some men a forward motion love,
But I by backward steps would move,   30
And when this dust falls to the urn
In that state I came return.

Silence, and stealth of days!

Silence, and stealth of days! 'tis now
                    Since thou art gone,
Twelve hundred hours, and not a brow
                    But clouds hang on.
As he that in some cave's thick damp   5
                    Locked from the light,
Fixeth a solitary lamp,
                    To brave the night,
And walking from his sun, when past
                    That glimmering ray   10
Cuts through the heavy mists in haste
                    Back to his day,
So o'er fled minutes I retreat
                    Unto that hour
Which showed thee last, but did defeat   15

Thy light and power,
I search, and rack my soul to see
Those beams again,
But nothing but the snuff to me
Appeareth plain;   20
That dark and dead sleeps in its known
And common urn,
But those fled to their Maker's throne
There shine and burn;
O could I track them! but souls must   25
Track one the other,
And now the spirit, not the dust
Must be thy brother.
Yet I have one pearl by whose light
All things I see,   30
And in the heart of earth, and night
Find Heaven, and thee.

The World

1

I saw Eternity the other night
Like a great ring of pure and endless light,
All calm as it was bright,
And round beneath it, Time in hours, days, years
Driven by the spheres   5
Like a vast shadow moved, in which the world
And all her train were hurled;
The doting lover in his quaintest strain
Did there complain,
Near him, his lute, his fancy, and his flights,   10
Wit's sour delights,
With gloves and knots the silly snares of pleasure
Yet his dear treasure
All scattered lay, while he his eyes did pore
Upon a flower.   15

2

The darksome statesman hung with weights and woe
Like a thick midnight-fog moved there so slow
He did not stay nor go;
Condemning thoughts (like sad eclipses) scowl
Upon his soul,   20
And clouds of crying witnesses without
Pursued him with one shout.
Yet digged the mole, and lest his ways be found

Worked underground,
Where he did clutch his prey, but One did see   25
That policy,
Churches and altars fed him, perjuries
Were gnats and flies,
It rained about him blood and tears, but he
Drank them as free.   30

3

The fearful miser on a heap of rust
Sat pining all his life there, did scarce trust
His own hands with the dust,
Yet would not place one piece above, but lives
In fear of thieves.   35
Thousands there were as frantic as himself
And hugged each one his pelf,
The downright epicure placed Heaven in sense
And scorned pretence
While others slipped into a wide excess   40
Said little less;
The weaker sort slight, trivial wares enslave
Who think them brave,
And poor, despised Truth sat counting by
Their victory.   45

4

Yet some, who all this while did weep and sing,
And sing and weep, soared up into the ring,
But most would use no wing.
O fools (said I) thus to prefer dark night
Before true light,   50
To live in grots, and caves, and hate the day
Because it shows the way,
The way which from this dead and dark abode
Leads up to God,
A way where you might tread the sun, and be   55
More bright than he.
But as I did their madness so discuss
One whispered thus –
"This ring the bride-groom did for none provide
But for his bride."   60

All that is in the world, the lust of the flesh, the lust of the eyes, and the pride of life, is not of the father, but is of the world. And the world passeth away, and the lusts thereof, but he that doth the will of God abideth for ever (1 John 2. 16–17).

I walked the other day (to spend my hour)

1

I walked the other day (to spend my hour)
    Into a field
Where I sometimes had seen the soil to yield
    A gallant flower,
But winter now had ruffled all the bower   5
    And curious store
    I knew there heretofore.

2

Yet I whose search loved not to peep and peer
    In the face of things
Thought with myself, there might be other springs   10
    Besides this here
Which, like cold friends, sees us but once a year,
    And so the flower
    Might have some other bower.

3

Then taking up what I could nearest spy   15
    I digged about
That place where I had seen him to grow out,
    And by and by
I saw the warm recluse alone to lie
    Where fresh and green   20
    He lived of us unseen.

4

Many a question intricate and rare
    Did I there strow,
But all I could extort was, that he now
    Did there repair   25
Such losses as befell him in this air
    And would ere long
    Come forth most fair and young.

5

This past, I threw the clothes quite o'er his head,
    And stung with fear   30
Of my own frailty dropped down many a tear
    Upon his bed,
Then sighing whispered, "Happy are the dead!
    What peace doth now
    Rock him asleep below?"   35

6

And yet, how few believe such doctrine springs
        From a poor root
Which all the winter sleeps here under foot
        And hath no wings
To raise it to the truth and light of things,   40
        But is still trod
        By every wandering clod.

7

O thou! whose spirit did at first inflame
        And warm the dead,
And by a sacred incubation fed   45
        With life this frame
Which once had neither being, form, nor name,
        Grant I may so
        Thy steps track here below,

8

That in these masques and shadows I may see   50
        Thy sacred way,
And by those hid ascents climb to that day
        Which breaks from thee
Who art in all things, though invisibly;
        Show me thy peace,   55
        Thy mercy, love, and ease,

9

And from this cave, where dreams and sorrows reign
        Lead me above
Where light, joy, leisure, and true comforts move
        Without all pain,   60
There, hid in thee, show me his life again
        At whose dumb urn
        Thus all the year I mourn.

They are all gone into the world of light!

They are all gone into the world of light!
        And I alone sit lingering here;
Their very memory is fair and bright,
        And my sad thoughts doth clear.

It glows and glitters in my cloudy breast   5
        Like stars upon some gloomy grove,
Or those faint beams in which this hill is dressed
        After the sun's remove.

I see them walking in an air of glory
    Whose light doth trample on my days –   10
My days, which are at best but dull and hoary,
    Mere glimmering and decays.

O holy Hope! and high Humility,
    High as the heavens above!
These are your walks, and you have showed them me   15
    To kindle my cold love,

Dear, beauteous Death! the jewel of the just,
    Shining nowhere but in the dark;
What mysteries do lie beyond thy dust;
    Could man outlook that mark!   20

He that hath found some fledged bird's nest may know
    At first sight if the bird be flown;
But what fair well, or grove he sings in now,
    That is to him unknown.

And yet, as angels in some brighter dreams   25
    Call to the soul, when man doth sleep,
So some strange thoughts transcend our wonted themes,
    And into glory peep.

If a star were confined into a tomb
    Her captive flames must needs burn there;   30
But when the hand that locked her up, gives room,
    She'll shine through all the sphere.

O Father of eternal life, and all
    Created glories under thee!
Resume thy spirit from this world of thrall   35
    Into true liberty.

Either disperse these mists, which blot and fill
    My perspective (still) as they pass,
Or else remove me hence unto that hill,
    Where I shall need no glass.   40

Thomas Traherne
(1637–1674)

Eden

A learned and happy ignorance
        Divided me
      From all the vanity,
From all the sloth, care, sorrow, that advance
    The madness and the misery   5
Of men. No error, no distraction, I
Saw cloud the earth, or overcast the sky.

I knew not that there was a serpent's sting,
        Whose poison shed
      On men did overspread   10
The world, nor did I dream of such a thing
    As sin, in which mankind lay dead.
They all were brisk and living things to me,
Yea, pure and full of immortality.

Joy, pleasure, beauty, kindness, charming love,   15
        Sleep, life, and light,
      Peace, melody—my sight,
Mine ears, and heart did fill and freely move;
    All that I saw did me delight;
The universe was then a world of treasure,   20
To me an universal world of pleasure.

Unwelcome penitence I then thought not on;
        Vain costly toys,
      Swearing and roaring boys,
Shops, markets, taverns, coaches, were unknown,   25
    So all things were that drown my joys;
No thorns choked up my path, nor hid the face
Of bliss and glory, nor eclipsed my place.

Only what Adam in his first estate,
        Did I behold;   30
      Hard silver and dry gold
As yet lay underground; my happy fate

Was more acquainted with the old
And innocent delights which he did see
In his original simplicity.   35

Those things which first his Eden did adorn,
   My infancy
  Did crown; simplicity
Was my protection when I first was born.
  Mine eyes those treasures first did see   40
Which God first made; the first effects of love
My first enjoyments upon earth did prove,

And were so great, and so divine, so pure,
   So fair and sweet,
  So true, when I did meet   45
Them here at first they did my soul allure,
  And drew away mine infant feet
Quite from the works of men, that I might see
The glorious wonders of the Deity.

Innocence

1

But that which most I wonder at, which most
I did esteem my bliss, which most I boast,
And ever shall enjoy, is that within
  I felt no stain, nor spot of sin.

  No darkness then did overshade,   5
  But all within was pure and bright,
  No guilt did crush, nor fear invade
  But all my soul was full of light.

  A joyful sense and puritie
   Is all I can remember.   10
  The very night to me was bright,
  Twas summer in December.

2

A serious meditation did employ
My soul within, which taken up with joy
Did seem no outward thing to note, but flie   15
  All objects that do feed the eye.

  While it those very objects did
  Admire, and prize, and praise, and love,
  Which in their glory most are hid,
  Which presence only doth remove.   20

Their constant daily presence I
    rejoicing at, did see;
And that which takes them from the iye
Of others, offered them to me.

3

No inward inclination did I feel   25
To avarice or pride: my soul did kneel
In admiration all the day. No lust nor strife
    Polluted then my infant life.

No fraud nor anger in me moved
No malice, jealousie or spite;   30
All that I saw I truly loved.
Contentment only and delight

Were in my soul. O Heav'n! what bliss
    Did I enjoy and feel!
What powerfull delight did this   35
Inspire! for this I daily kneel.

4

Whether it be that Nature is so pure,
And custom only vicious; or that sure
God did by miracle the guilt remove,
    And make my soul to feel his Love,   40

So early: or that 'twas one day,
Wher in this happiness I found;
Whose strength and brightness so do ray,
That still it seemeth to surround.

What ere it is, it is a light   45
    So endless unto me
That I a world of true delight
Did then and to this day do see.

5

That prospect was the gate of Heav'n, that day
The ancient light of Eden did convey   50
Into my soul: I was an Adam there,
    A little Adam in a sphere

Of joys! O there my ravisht sense
Was entertained in Paradise,
And had a sight of innocence.   55
All was beyond all bound and price.

An antepast of Heaven sure!
    I on the earth did reign.

Within, without me, all was pure.
I must become a child again.   60

My Spirit

1

My naked simple life was I.
         That act so strongly shined
Upon the earth, the sea, the skie,
It was the substance of my mind.
         The sense it self was I.   5
I felt no dross nor matter in my soul,
No brims nor borders, such as in a bowl
We see, my essence was capacitie.
                  That felt all things,
                     The thought that springs   10
Therfrom's itself. It hath no other wings
         To spread abroad, nor eyes to scc,
                  Nor hands distinct to feel,
                     Nor knees to kneel:
But being simple like the deitie   15
         In its own centre is a sphere
         Not shut up here, but every where.

2

         It acts not from a centre to
                  Its object as remote,
         But present is, when it doth view,   20
         Being with the being it doth note.
                  Whatever it doth do,
It doth not by another engine work,
But by itself; which in the act doth lurk.
Its essence is transformed into a true   25
                  And perfect act.
                  And so exact
Hath God appeard in this mysterious fact,
         That tis all eye, all act, all sight,
                  And what it pleas can be,   30
                  Not only see,
Or do; for tis more voluble than light:
         Which can put on ten thousand forms,
         Being clothed with what itself adorns.

3

This made me present evermore   35
         With whatso ere I saw.
An object, if it were before

My eye, was by dame Nature's Law,
Within my soul. Her store
Was all at once within me; all her treasures   40
Were my immediate and internal pleasures,
Substantial joys, which did inform my mind.
With all she wrought,
My soul was fraught,
And every object in my soul a thought   45
Begot, or was; I could not tell,
Whether the things did there
Themselves appear,
Which in my spirit *truly* seemed to dwell;
Or whether my conforming mind   50
Were not even all that therein shind.

4

But yet of this I was most sure,
That at the utmost length,
(So worthy was it to endure)
My soul could best express its strength,   55
It was so quick and pure,
That all my mind was wholly every where
What ere it saw, twas ever wholy there;
The sun ten thousand legions off, was nigh:
The utmost star,   60
Tho seen from far,
Was present in the apple of my eye.
There was my sight, my life, my sense,
My substance and my mind
My spirit shined   65
Even there, not by a transeunt influence.
The act was immanent, yet there.
The thing remote, yet felt even here.

5

O Joy! O wonder, and delight!
O sacred mysterie!   70
My soul a spirit infinite!
An image of the deitie!
A pure substantiall light!
That being greatest which doth nothing seem!
Why, twas my All, I nothing did esteem   75
But that alone. A strange mysterious sphere!
A deep abyss
That sees and is
The only proper place or Bower of Bliss.
To its creator tis so near   80
In love and excellence

In life and sense,
In greatness worth and nature; and so dear;
    In it, without hyperbole,
        The son and friend of God we see.   85

                    6
        A strange extended orb of joy,
            Proceeding from within,
        Which did on every side convey
            Itself, and being nigh of kin
                To God did every way   90
Dilate it self even in an instant, and
Like an indivisible centre stand
At once surrounding all eternitie.
            'Twas not a sphere
                Yet did appear   95
One infinite. Twas somewhat everywhere.
        And tho it had a power to see
            Far more, yet still it shind
                And was a mind
Exerted† for it saw infinitie   100
        Twas not a sphere, but twas a power
            Invisible, and yet a bower.

                    7
        O wondrous self! O sphere of light,
            O sphere of joy most fair;
        O act, O power infinite;   105
        O subtile, and unbounded air!
            O living orb of sight!
Thou which within me art, yet me! Thou eye,
And temple of his whole infinitie!
O what a world art thou! a world within!   110
            All things appear,
            All objects are
Alive in thee! supersubstancial, rare,
        Above them selves, and nigh of kin
            To those pure things we find   115
            In his great mind
Who made the world! tho now ecclypsd by sin.
        There they are usefull and divine,
            Exalted there they ought to shine.

Index of Titles and First Lines